Cassoulet Confessions

Award-winning food and travel writer Sylvie Bigar was born in Geneva, Switzerland, and lives in New York City. Her writing has appeared widely, including in *The New York Times*, *The Washington Post*, *Food & Wine*, *Forbes.com*, *Saveur*, *Bon Appetit*, *Edible*, *Departures*, *Travel & Leisure* and *National Geographic Traveler*. In French, Sylvie has contributed to *Le Figaro*, *Histoire Magazine*, *Le Temps* and *FrenchMorning.com*.

*Some names have been changed to protect
the privacy of the people involved.*

Cassoulet Confessions

Food, France, Family,
and the Stew
That Saved My Soul

Sylvie Bigar

Hardie Grant

BOOKS

Published in 2022 by Hardie Grant Books,
an imprint of Hardie Grant Publishing

Hardie Grant Books (Melbourne)
Wurundjeri Country
Building 1, 658 Church Street
Richmond, Victoria 3121

Hardie Grant Books (London)
5th & 6th Floors
52–54 Southwark Street
London SE1 1UN

hardiegrantbooks.com

Excerpt from *Beans, A History* by Ken Albala, © Ken Albala, reproduced
with permission.

Quotations from the following publications have been used, with thanks:
Histoire Comique by Anatole France and *The Occitan Feast* by Prosper
Montagné.

Every effort has been made to trace, contact and acknowledge all copyright
holders. Please contact the publisher with any information on errors
or omissions.

A catalogue record for this
book is available from the
National Library of Australia

Cassoulet Confessions
ISBN 978 1 74379 796 9

10 9 8 7 6 5 4 3 2 1

Cover design by Emily O'Neill
Text design by Emily O'Neill
Typeset in Granjon by Emily O'Neill
Printed in Spain by Estellaprint

The product has been awarded EU Ecolabel Licence No FI/011/007 and is
Nordic Ecolabel Inspected Paper

Hardie Grant acknowledges the Traditional Owners of the country on which
we work, the Wurundjeri people of the Kulin nation and the Gadigal people
of the Eora nation, and recognises their continuing connection to the land,
waters and culture. We pay our respects to their Elders past and present.

Contents

To my beloved parents

Prologue

WOBBLY FROM ALMOST TWENTY HOURS OF TRAVEL, I SWUNG open the metallic doors of the restaurant kitchen, put my bag down and stopped short. On the counter, next to the neatly folded apron and the heavy knife, a pig's head stared me down with sad eyes filled with eternity.

In my mind, I could still hear my six-year-old daughter Zoe's squeal as I attempted to embrace her. She squirmed and pushed me away.

'No, Maman, don't leave!' she wailed.

My husband Michael knelt on the carpet and held her as he waved me on, smiling bravely as our four-year-old son ran around the living room singing 'Ring Around the Rosie'. Filled with both piercing guilt and elation, I took a deep breath, turned around, closed the front door behind me and headed to the airport.

It was April 2008 and I was a Swiss-French food and travel writer based in New York City. Months earlier, I had been discussing a story idea with a magazine editor for whom I tracked down unsung cooks, forgotten spices, and secret culinary traditions. 'Here,' I'd said, as we pored over the map of France, my index finger wedged between Spain and Provence, over a French region named Occitanie – at the crossroads of history and civilizations.

'The local specialty is cassoulet,' I continued. 'An ancestral meat and bean stew I hear tastes like velvet cocoa. The locals speak a mysterious language; they spread bizarre legends.'

'Go,' was all he said.

I exhaled. My editor had just handed me the perfect escape: a few days of solo travel through France with a delicious purpose. Truth be told, I had been dying to take a break from what may have looked like the perfect urban picket fence life.

I'd grown up alongside two older sisters with disabilities, within a wealthy but wildly dysfunctional family, and had sworn I would never have children. I managed to sail through my first marriage without diverting from that credo, but a year into my second, I woke up one morning with a bad case of nesting fever. Perhaps, I thought, I could placate this new craving by adopting a dog. But once we brought Chocolat – named for the chocolate croissants of my childhood – home from the pound, the fierce love I felt for him just made me crave a deeper connection. It was as if this puppy opened in me a door I hadn't known existed. Beyond that door hid a person I'd never met. A person who stopped taking the pill after twenty years of steady use, got pregnant a few days later and would spend the next nine months on an ecstatic trip, convinced that she had morphed into a magical vessel of life. One child turned out to be not enough. A year after my daughter was born, while leukemia gnawed at my beloved father, I became pregnant with a son.

Fast forward a few years, I was writing more about food than travel and had turned into a stroller-pushing Upper West Side Mama. A Mama who was dying to escape.

❧

Which explains why from my home in New York City, I flew to Paris and on to Toulouse, where I caught a rickety train, beige paint peeling from its flanks, bound for magical, medieval Carcassonne and its fifty-two towers.

Pre-kids, I'd traveled widely. In Marseilles, I'd gotten high on bouillabaisse, the wildly fragrant fish and shellfish stew; in Strasbourg, I'd almost lost my heart to an Alsatian chef and his rustic choucroute, and in Dijon I lathered so much mustard on roast beef that the pile on my plate became known locally as a mustard sandwich. It was high time to dig into Occitanie's cassoulet, the slow-cooked carnivorous orgy of pork, lamb, duck, beans, and herbs stewed together in an earthenware tureen. The same dish that had been dubbed 'the God of Occitan cuisine' by Prosper Montagné, who in 1938 penned the *Larousse Gastronomique*, the first encyclopedia of French recipes, culinary terms, and techniques.

More research revealed that cassoulet, it seemed, had spurred a whole religion. In 1990, chef Eric Garcia of Domaine Balthazar near Carcassonne rallied a local group made up of activist chefs, fervent foodies, and vibrant vintners. Horrified by the mounting tide of 'all-you-can-eat-cassoulet for eight euros' that threatened the region – and possibly the world – they founded an association they named, simply, *L'Académie Universelle du Cassoulet*. No local or national modesty here; its crucial mission had to be universal: preserve and defend the ancestral dish.

That sounded like my kind of battle. A band of toque-wearing Davids rallying against the Goliaths of mass tourism and culinary debacle in defense of a mythical stew. A quick, fun story, I thought. I couldn't have been more wrong.

1

Geneva, summer 1970

WE NEVER ATE CASSOULET AT BEAU-CHAMP, MY SWISS childhood home above Lake Geneva. We didn't eat lentils either, or any other mundane legumes for that matter, but Joachim Martinez, our loyal Spanish butler, served us plenty of *haricots verts*, glistening with French butter and dotted with caramelized shallots. Some days he wore his royal blue jacket with gold buttons, some days he wore the red, but he always wore his white gloves as he slalomed swiftly around the oval table.

'Joachim,' my mother would say, 'help the little one, please.'

'*Oui*, madame.'

That little one was me, age seven or so, with my round face and corkscrew curls. I had recently graduated from eating in the upstairs kitchenette, with its red linoleum floor and arthritic dumbwaiter, to the dining room, where I sat proudly to the right of my mother and across from my three older sisters.

Joachim, stocky, with warm brown eyes and a bushy mustache vaguely reminiscent of Francisco Franco's, held his right arm behind his back when he waited on us, as any proper butler would. His hefty left palm cradled one of the oval silver platters he shined regularly, and as he approached my left side, he would bend his knees to lower himself. Right hand wielding both utensils with the precision of a surgeon, he would serve me, lest I dropped a morsel on the oriental carpet. He knew I preferred the crispy chunks near the top of the lamb bone, the chicken drumsticks wrapped in brittle skin, and the fluffy knöpfli his wife Carmela made from my maternal grandmother's recipe. Aware my parents insisted I try everything, he would pick for me the thinnest endive, which I'd try to wedge under the bones, and only a sprinkling of *petits pois*, whose texture always made me gag.

Dinner was a serious affair. Not so much because my parents cared about how the food tasted (more on that later), but because the dining room felt as convivial as a pretty morgue. Decorated with wood paneling painted off-beige and featuring a centuries-old parquet floor, the room had been styled by my father with furniture and objects he inherited from what we all called 'Rue Saint-Victor', the mansion on Saint-Victor Street where he grew up, about ten miles away in downtown Geneva.

Often bored by the conversation between my parents, I entertained myself by detailing the eighteenth-century Meissen porcelain birds that adorned the walls. Each panel held about three of them, for a total of twenty-one. None seemed happy or chirpy – quite the opposite. One was picking at a smaller dead one, another gnawed on a worm, and the one across from me was chasing a squirrel. The birds looked mean and ominous.

'I hated those damn birds,' my mother would say years later, as if I should have always known that. But I didn't. There was much I didn't know then.

Built on a hill in 1730 by a Swiss nobleman, our neoclassical stone château, with its sculpted gable and gray shutters, occupied about 15,000 square feet, and was divided into three floors. It overlooked a vast garden separated into two distinct parts by a low stone wall lined with red roses. Every day, our gardener fought to keep the formal upper area meticulously clean-cut. Week after week, he battled against the foolish weeds on the gravel paths that lined the gardens; year after year, he braided climbing roses over undulating wrought-iron arches and kept the ancient water basin impeccably rimmed with rows of lavender. But below, the field for which the house was named (*beau champ* means beautiful meadow) cascaded towards the lake into wilderness. It was the domain of the ladybugs and the bees, where tall grasses and wildflowers bowed to the morning breeze, where I ran free and where I hid. There, the white bottom of the clover flower tasted sweet and I could make the swollen buds of the campions explode like firecrackers in my able hands.

In my favorite imaginary game, I was a squirrel, stocking provisions away for winter. I collected a whole array of leaves, acorns, unripe chestnuts, and white pebbles I would hide in the numerous caches the garden provided. I kept mental lists of what was where: between the roots of the oldest pine tree, under a funny-shaped stone or a cluster of ivy. Was I squirreling away my childhood for fear of forgetting it, or was I actually afraid I'd go hungry?

At the head of the table, my father, trim and tanned, faced the two monumental windows.

'Look at the way Norbert steers,' he whispered one day, frowning, his piercing hazel eyes on the lake where a lone sailboat flew, its spinnaker billowing in the north wind.

SYLVIE BIGAR

'Oh, really? How can you tell from here?' asked my mother, not looking.

My father had been sailing competitively every weekend since he was a teenager and, even from miles away, he could recognize who steered which craft and how. His first 'boat' was built at age eight using a lone board, a broom, and a sheet he'd borrowed from the housekeeper at Le Clapotis, the lake chalet his parents owned, only a few minutes' walk from our own home on the hill.

He stared at my mother and didn't respond. At the beginning of their forty-year marriage, he'd tried to share his passion with his young Parisian bride, but after a few outings during which my dainty, intellectual mother became seasick, she decided she'd rather be reading.

I watched the lake, as alive as the ocean. Across the water, the countryside seemed to stretch up in escalating tiers towards the French pre-Alps. Above, the steady snowy summit of Mont Blanc, the highest peak in Europe, floated high, placid, above our lives.

If rays of sun deigned to enter the dining room, my father would often shudder. 'Quick, Joachim, close the curtains,' he'd cry, seriously upset. He loved the intricate eighteen-century parquets and the oriental rug, and feared the sun's deadly rays, even though once the yellowing 'anti-sun' curtains were drawn, the room felt more like a funeral parlor.

'Jeanine, elbows off the table!' he'd yell suddenly. 'Two points!'

Her clear blue eyes shining with fury, my oldest sister would stare at him. 'I am almost twenty and you're going to send me to my room if I get to three points?'

He'd laugh, but the tension was palpable. Our father was obsessed with manners. He had invented a 'game' he played with my three sisters before I was born in which any infraction resulted in a point.

8

Three points and you would be sent to your room without dinner.

When I was born, my sisters were already eight, ten, and twelve years old: they never pardoned me. By the time I sat at the dining table with them, they were young adults, but I'd heard about many meals where Jeanine and France would finish the evening hungry, sobbing in their rooms. I was often threatened with the points game, but I was never sent away. I never went hungry.

After they left home – Jeanine to get married, France to live her Israeli kibbutz dream, and Michèle in a straightjacket, en route to the mental hospital – I was mostly alone at the table with my parents.

Was that when I started to notice that my mother ate differently from us? That while we lapped a cream of asparagus, she sipped clear vegetable broth; that her sole filet was steamed while ours was fried?

2

New York, February 2008

AS I PREPARED FOR THE TRIP, CURLED UP IN MY HOME OFFICE in New York, I googled Eric Garcia, co-founder of the *Académie Universelle du Cassoulet*. To my surprise, the search generated a long list of hits. A blurry photo showed him sitting at a long table amongst other chefs, seemingly a judge at what looked like a formal culinary competition. Everyone else was dressed in chef whites and toques, but he wore a simple black shirt, giving him the air of a workman. A yellow, perfectly sharpened pencil emerged from behind his ear. Middle-aged, graying, thick around the middle, this man could pass for a favorite uncle if it wasn't for the intensity of his stare. I was drawn in. There was inner purpose here, someone who didn't need a uniform to prove his craft or his stature.

L'Express, the French equivalent of *Newsweek,* had dubbed him 'The Pope of Cassoulet'. Asked when he'd first cooked the dish, he'd answered without missing a beat: 'March 19, 1960! I peeled a whole mountain of garlic for what was considered, at the time, a pauper's dish.'

I would learn later that his father, a Spanish shepherd, fled the iron rule of Franco's dictatorship in 1939 by walking across the Pyrenees, the mountain range that separates France from Spain. At the time, about 500,000 Republican refugees fled Spain in the dead of winter while under attack from Nationalists and Italian planes, a little-discussed exodus that would become known as *La Retirada*, the retreat. Garcia was one of seven children, and money was sparse. 'My mother made delicious food with very little,' he'd said. 'Instead of telling us she was making a paella, she would say she was making a rice.' Garcia was only fourteen when he was hired to peel potatoes and carrots in the basement of a local inn. After about a year, he was allowed to climb up to the kitchen. There, he found his calling.

From kitchen to kitchen, he fought his way through, always ready for another twelve-hour day on his feet, another shift, a new trick to learn from a colleague. While his friends spent their hard-earned money on girls and beer, he'd stay in his room and save his francs to buy cookbooks. His first acquisition was the 1938 *Larousse Gastronomique*, the 1206-page food encyclopedia Garcia called 'the manifesto of French cuisine'. He often quoted from it and was known to quiz culinary students about its more obscure references. 'Where did the apricot tree originate? What's different about the way blue cheese matures? What is the soul of choucroute?' He knew the entire book by heart, it seemed.

Asked in another interview about his many years at The Negresco, the historic Michelin-starred hotel and restaurant in Nice on the French Riviera (whose cupola was rumored to have been modeled on the breast of the owner's mistress), he said, 'When

I landed at The Negresco, I thought I'd arrived. In fact, even though I'd been cooking for ten years, I was back to being a commis, meaning everyone's servant.' It would take him fifteen years to rise from servant to sous-chef under celebrity chef Jacques Maximin.

In the end, it was his native land's mermaid call that convinced Garcia to leave Nice's palm trees and glamor behind and head home to Carcassonne. In 1995, he bought a crumbling domaine complete with a twelfth-century tower a few miles outside Carcassonne's walls. He and his wife Laurence completely renovated the structure, replanted the garden and opened a restaurant they named Domaine Balthazar.

Only about three hours by car from Provence to the east and Barcelona to the south, the local terroir combined fragrant lavender fields and tangy rosemary bushes, sweet Mediterranean seabass and fiery garlicky shrimp, washed down with a wide palette of unsung southwestern wines. Garcia translated the region onto his short menu – confit of lamb shoulder with wild thyme; just-seared duck foie gras with roasted figs. But the true star was cassoulet, whose centuries-old recipe Garcia had perfected to the point where it immediately became iconic.

'Cassoulet has fostered its own religion,' Garcia told *Time* magazine. 'Because it's the *plat de partage* – the epitome of the convivial dish. When a cassoulet lands on the table, bubbling with delicious aromas, something magical happens – it's Communion at the table.'

In a recent interview in local paper *La Dépêche*, Garcia ranted against the proliferation of the cheap, all-you-can-eat cassoulet that certain eateries offered innocent tourists for eight euros. He sounded out of control, dangerous almost. I could practically hear his outrage. His passion was contagious. I found the number of his restaurant and called.

After three rings a woman answered.

'*Domaine Balthazar, bonjour,*' came a singsong greeting.

'Could I please speak with Monsieur Garcia?' I asked, in French.

'*Un instant.*'

'*Allo, oui,*' came a different voice, this one male and resonant.

I introduced myself and explained the reason for my call. I said that I was from New York, working as a writer and soon to visit the region. I stressed my interest in cassoulet, its history, the ingredients. How was it made? What made it special? I went on. He cut me off.

'A journalist-a frrrromeh Nooo Yok *who speaks French?*' he chanted in the melodious and elongated accent of the South of France. 'Come for lunch on Sunday.' And, just like that, he hung up. It felt more like a summons than an invitation, but I guessed it would do.

I often traveled between New York and Geneva, where my mother still lived in the family manor, but there was no way to arrive for lunch in Carcassonne without leaving two days prior. A few weeks later, I landed at Charles de Gaulle airport in Paris after a short night on the plane. As soon as I stepped out of the gangway, I was hit with what felt like a buttery cloud. I'd left Newark's food courts behind and arrived directly at Ladurée, a pastry shop founded in 1863! On the other side of the terminal, travelers were lining up for croissants from Paul, a bakery established in 1889. That afternoon, after just an hour in the air, I found myself in Toulouse, often dubbed the Pink City for its unique reddish-pink clay brick buildings. A taxi took me to the train station. Carcassonne was only two hours away.

There are two Carcassonnes. One is a small typical French town with a pedestrian main street called Rue de la République and the ubiquitous Place du Général du Gaulle, a massive square where farmers and artisans flock every Saturday for the weekly greenmarket. Then there's the walled marvel locals refer to as *La Cité*.

I emerged bleary-eyed from the tiny train station and walked across the bridge over the historic Canal du Midi. Built in 1681 under Louis XIV, the 120-mile Canal du Midi slices France in two, connecting the Atlantic Ocean to the Mediterranean Sea. Bordered on both sides by age-old plane trees, it boasts ninety-one locks. I'd heard that cruising on the canal on slow-moving barges meant taking a trip into an impressionist landscape.

I took a taxi towards what looked like a gigantic floating fort. Restored by nineteenth-century architect Viollet-le-Duc and often decried as inauthentic, La Cité and its fifty-two towers resembled Cinderella's castle. I let myself get transported to another world. After checking into my hotel, I spent the afternoon strolling around, exploring the towers and the monuments, dodging the crowds, biding my time. I imagined soldiers in full armor, merchants accosting women on market day, traveling musicians walking on the cobblestone lanes, their instrument cases across their backs. As the sun set, Carcassonne shed its tourists one by one through the drawbridge. I stayed.

Someone from the Academy was supposed to meet me the next morning. When the alarm sounded at ten, my body rebelled, knowing it was only four in the morning. Coffee and breakfast helped. Suddenly, preceded by a terribly potent mustache that did its best to hide a wide smile, a man appeared before me.

'Bonjour, mademoiselle, Alfred Tarena!' he trumpeted, his wide paw crushing my hand.

His name sounded like a cannonade. He introduced himself as the Under Secretary of the Academy, dispatched to pick me up. A barrel-chested insurance agent in his late forties, Tarena divided his free time between his two passions, rugby and cassoulet. Tarena escorted me to his car and we drove out in the direction of the Domaine, Garcia's stronghold.

3

Carcassonne, April 2008

COME FOR LUNCH, HE'D SAID. AT DOMAINE BALTHAZAR, weeks after my initial call and 3782 miles from New York, lunch burst through the door with as much pomp as could be mustered by a group of meaty, middle-aged oompa-loompas ambling into the dining room dressed in scarlet robes with billowy sleeves, yellow ribbon tied at the neck.

This was not the simple Sunday lunch I thought I had been summoned to. Everything spoke of ritual, of tradition, of ceremony. The dresses, red with white trim, matched by soft, beret-style caps, reminded me of academics in graduation processions. Miniature versions of the *cassole*, the terracotta pot that provided the basis for the name cassoulet, hung on green ribbons around thick tan necks, like medals of honor. Men and women sang in a mysterious language as they marched out of the kitchen.

And this parade had a float. A centerpiece shaped like a stretcher and framed by two elongated poles made of raw wood held a platform fashioned from planks. From the side hung a red satin banner with gold fringes, emblazoned with the words *Académie Universelle du Cassoulet*. Resting on the platform, presented with a pride ordinarily reserved for an infant prince, was a pair of gargantuan *cassoles* too big for me to wrap with my biggest bear hug. Each end of the stretcher was gripped by a man in a robe. The procession streamed into the dining room.

The bouncy beat of their singing sounded like a folk song, or maybe some sort of anthem. I tried to make out the lyrics then, recognizing none of the words, tried to place the language. French? No, I knew the singing was not in *ma langue maternelle*, my mother tongue. It was not in Italian, the other language I spoke, nor in English. I could usually distinguish Spanish, German, and bits and pieces of other languages, but this was unlike anything I had ever heard.

I would soon learn that the language was Occitan, a medieval romance language indigenous to southern France and northern Spain. I would also learn the French version of the tune, as well as its translation:

Rediscover in cassoulet
The taste of simplicity. The taste of truth.
Respect the art, respect the tradition.
Simmer, oh simmer hour after hour.
Break the crust, carefully, time after time
Burning your fingertips, just a tiny bit.

But in the moment, in that overstimulating, overwhelming moment, all I could manage was a bit of marvel and a lot of wonder. Where the hell was I?

I tried to take it all in. Earth-toned tiles and salmon-colored curtains gave the room a warm if somewhat rustic atmosphere, which contrasted with the elegance of the impeccably pressed white tablecloth. Had I been invited to a banquet? Looking down, I found a beige china plate flanked by two forks on the left and two knives on the right. Above the plate, a spoon rested next to a roll of crusty bread. Four wine glasses anchored each setting. There were no water glasses. I counted about twenty guests, but I was the only one not singing.

I watched the parade circle the table for the three minutes it took to complete the song. The group came to a stop opposite me. It took two members of the robed fraternity to lift the pot from the platform and place what was obviously the guest of honor on a silver tray on the table. I rose to get a better view. Peering down into the *cassole*, I saw a bubbling, golden crust.

Holding a massive wooden spoon as long as his arm, Garcia stood still, ready to pounce.

'*Allez*!' he eructed suddenly.

As with a javelin, he jabbed into the living, bubbly crust, releasing a fog of fumes. I almost felt the blow and winced, wondering if the thing was going to explode. Two large dollops of what looked like supersized beans, duck meat, and sausage, moist with shiny, unapologetic fat, landed on my plate. I couldn't wait. I scooped a bite and lifted it to my lips.

They all stared ('the American didn't even wait for us to be served,' someone whispered), but I couldn't see. I'd closed my eyes.

Home, I thought, shuddering. This is the taste of home.

It didn't make any sense.

4

Geneva, 1970s

'YOU LIVE HERE?' MY CLASSMATES ASKED AS THEY TIPTOED onto the pink and gray marble checked floor. Their necks would twist up and their eyes would travel towards the immense Middle Ages tapestry, with its vaguely obscene hunting theme, that hung along the grand staircase.

My parents already had two daughters, Jeanine and France, and one more on the way when they realized their two-bedroom apartment in the center of Geneva would soon be too small. My father's engineering practice was successful, and he was starting to make a name for himself as a real-estate developer. His passion for sailing and his love of the lake brought him to Gothange, the small village on a hill overlooking the natural harbor where, at age eight, he'd built his first sailboat.

'There's only one house for sale in Gothange and it's not for you,

Frédéric,' said Thierry Devrest, a long-time family friend and real-estate broker. 'It's way too big.'

That was exactly the kind of thing to tell Frédéric Adler if you wanted to spark his interest. I can just picture how his bushy left eyebrow must have shot right up as he turned to Devrest with a sarcastic smile.

'Too big? Why?'

Devrest tells of driving to the house and parking just next to the church. Uninvited and undeterred by the rusty wrought-iron gate he pushed open, my father strode inside the finely graveled courtyard – he didn't ring the bell – and walked determinedly around the gray stone manor. He reached the stone terrace, stopped short and stared ahead. The day was clear. The next time, he rang the bell. He bought the house a few weeks later. Too big, my mother had protested, way too big, but what she said never really mattered to him.

In a letter he wrote to me while I was studying in New York, he told me that as a child, he used to stroll with his parents along one of the roads that borders the property. 'On summer evenings, fifty years ago,' he wrote, 'my parents and I often walked up from the Creux-de-Gothange, where we rented a chalet, towards the village on the hill. This mysterious, dark garden felt both magical, since it only existed for me during summer vacation, and safe, since I experienced these strolls with my parents, the epitome of safety.'

I don't actually remember the first time I became conscious of the view. The scenery was always there as the stunning backdrop to my childhood. And if the view was the stage, then the towering trees planted throughout the garden acted as nature's curtains, framing the lake. Many dated back to the eighteenth century, when the most famous owner of the house, a botanist and writer named Charles Bonnet, set out to plant rare specimens, composing a unique landscape.

Almost as famous as Bonnet was the impossibly tall tree, originally from South America, that we called the 'monkey tree'. I later discovered that its true name was *Araucaria*, and that its common nickname was devised because even for a monkey, climbing along the dangerous spiny leaves was impossible. But as a child I believed it held miniature monkeys, and that if I looked hard enough, I would discover one.

What I did see, one very early morning, was not a monkey but a naked man, watering our flower beds. Monsieur Despraz, a seemingly respectable, white-haired nature lover, had been our gardener for a few years already when I spotted him from my window, wearing nothing but a strange hose hanging from his tanned belly. Later that day, after his black moped disappeared through the gates, I ran to the shed at the far end of the garden and pried the metallic doors open. On the dusty bench was an old box. It took a while to get it to open but when I did, dozens of photos of naked women fell on the muddy floor. I had never seen anything similar. Making certain I was alone, I closed the accordion doors and sat down. By then I must have been about ten years old and my knowledge of sexuality was blurry at best. I was shocked but also excited somehow. I remember feeling that I looked nothing like these women. For sure, my body didn't hide parts like these. I put everything back the way I had found it and ran away. Did my parents know the gardener's secret? I never told.

5

Geneva, 1970s

AS A TEN YEAR OLD I SPENT COUNTLESS HOURS PLAYING IN the garden with Joachim Junior, also known as JJ to differentiate him from his formidable father. JJ was a year younger than me, thin and wiry, and his strict, Catholic parents kept his brown hair cropped. Even though we resided in the same house, our lives were utterly different. We both climbed the gnarly Catalpa, but I picked its long, green beans and pretended to cook a gigantic *salade niçoise* while he carved his name onto its venerable trunk with the tiny pocket knife he'd found in the front yard of the village school. He hid in the cluster of pine trees and threw pebbles at me, remaining invisible, hidden somewhere at the top of the thickest specimen. He played in the courtyard with toy cars. I sat at the center of the vast meadow and imagined I was an abandoned princess. At dinnertime we would both race to the house, but he always beat me to the side door, the one that led to the kitchen – his mother's domain – where the family would sit for their meals once, and only once, we were done eating.

My bedroom was on the second floor but his was on the third, under the roof. On Sundays he would disappear with his family for mysterious outings. I liked him, but it was clear he didn't reciprocate.

'You're ugly,' he'd say. I didn't believe him, but it still stung.

By July at Beau-Champ, the cluster of linden trees, 130 feet high perhaps, would start shedding their delicate flowers. Entranced by the mighty northern wind we called *la Bise* (pronounced beez), the delicate blossoms twirled around until most of them landed in a sort of kidney pool my father designed in the early sixties to resemble an uneven figure eight. Children played in the shallow small oval, which was separated from the larger oval by a concrete bridge built as an arch. Like a cloud of iridescent dragonflies, the flowers would carry on their wings their sweet, slightly lemony taste. For weeks after that, my sisters and I would not only be engulfed in linden vapors as we approached the pool area, we would bathe in them. The smaller basin lay closest to the trees, so that's where the infusion was strongest. It was also, of course, the warmest part of the pool, so we soaked in herbal tea.

Around the pool, a wide circle of concrete was studded with marble chunks, resulting in a modernist mosaic. A red brick pavilion, complete with changing rooms, bathrooms, and a kitchenette, supported a slightly concave concrete roof.

Once I was a teenager, I discovered how striking and unique this design was but, earlier, all I knew was that bathing in linden was delicious, jumping as far as I could from the bridge was daring, and if you managed to climb on the roof of the pavilion, you could sun, naked, far from all.

On the other side of the pool, two majestic cedars book-ended the terrace. The blue one, the tallest tree in the garden, stretched towards the summer sky, its smoky blue needles expanding until none of us could distinguish what was tree and what was azure. The other, a so-called Cedar of Lebanon, brought a welcome shade onto the stone bench that sprouted from the brick wall. I can still feel how hot that bench got in the summer, so hot we had to lay a towel over the scorching stone to be able to sit on it.

But the bench and this tree were also famous for a story I heard told numerous times during my childhood. One afternoon, my oldest sister Jeanine was seated on that bench, studying for a particularly arduous exam. She was so focused on her work that she didn't notice the sun was gone and a strong wind was blowing in from the lake. She paid no attention to the changing weather. Suddenly, lightning struck the tip of the tree, effectively slicing its trunk in two. Before Jeanine could even get up, half the cedar had landed around her. Miraculously, she was unharmed. It was this last part that was drilled repeatedly into my young mind: she could have died. Storms were dangerous and staying under a tree during a storm was something I should never do. In case of a storm, get up and run was the message – but there was more. What I heard was that the world was a dangerous place, and even within our magical garden, we were at risk.

Fear had entered my consciousness.

6

Carcassonne, April 2008

I OPENED MY EYES AND PUT MY FORK DOWN. THEY WERE still staring at me. What I had just tasted had nothing in common with any mundane stew I had experienced during my past travels through France. How could this even be called a stew? Each ingredient sang its own gustative melody. The beans, plump and creamy but still intact, seemed to have absorbed the grassy, floral essence of the bouquet garni – that bundle of fresh mountainous herbs and veggies – but also the earthy flavor of the meats. The duck was tender with thin crispy peaks, strands of pork melted in my mouth, and binding it all was what I could only describe as caramelized sensuality. It was, in fact, the crust of the cassoulet.

'*Délicieux!*' I shouted, throwing my arms in the air.

Berets went flying as the entire group jumped up and cheered before we toasted the cassoulet with a deep red wine from the nearby

Minervois region. Later, on my palate I recognized garlic, loads of fragrant garlic. The scent took me back to a conversation with Arianne, my best friend's mother, who as a young bride in tightfisted 1950s Geneva – the old Calvin stronghold – realized she was finally free to cook with garlic. In her parents' kitchen, the unwelcome bulb had been deemed vulgar, but she now used its sensual, smelly power as a means to celebrate her sexuality and her new culinary freedom. Every time she squeezed a clove out of its tight sock, she told me, she felt like a porn star.

There was more garlic in the crisp salad served in the terracotta bowls that made the rounds after the cassoulet, and by then I had sipped three different southern wines I never knew existed.

But what was this academy, I wondered. The French Hogwarts? The brotherhood of deliciousness? I would learn that, shedding any semblance of modesty, Garcia based his newborn association on the *Académie Française*, a body of literary authorities created in 1685 whose mission was (and still is) the safeguarding of the French language. His universal academy would safeguard cassoulet. Protect it. Defend it. Against whom? And why?

I vaguely remember someone offering rosemary sorbet and a sweet late-harvest muscat, but the rest of the day is a blur. I woke up the next morning with no memory of how I'd gotten from the restaurant back to the hotel. I looked out to a ribbon of ramparts studded by thin towers coiffed with red brick roofs; ancient stone walls peeking out from under blankets of ivy, and, beneath my window, a steady flow of tourists gawking at the medieval city.

The phone rang.

'*Sylvie, tu dors?*' said Garcia.

'No, I'm awake,' I responded, my mouth pasty.

'Ten minutes at the drawbridge. We have to talk.'

'*Oui*, chef.'

He'd already hung up. I rushed to get ready and, asking for directions, ran as best I could with my flats on the cobblestone paths all the way to the entrance of the fortress. He was waiting, *bien sûr*.

'Slept well?' he asked with a mischievous smile.

'*Oui, merci.*'

As he kissed me on the cheeks, he seemed to tower over me, but the bulk of the force I felt came mostly from his torso. His arms and shoulders spoke of heavy pots and quivering animals butchered at dawn. I dug into his dark, piercing eyes and saw both an iron will and a tender heart.

His Renault's square contours suggested a 1970s vintage. Faded black paint and dozens of dings were testimony to decades of driving the region's sun-soaked roads. Inside, the smell of dried blood told of the carcasses of beasts being lugged from local farms to the kitchen.

'*On y va?*' he said.

'Let's go,' I replied.

We crossed another bridge, this one towards the 'new' town, and drove out through sunflower fields.

'You have a lot to learn, *ma petite*,' he said. 'Cassoulet is more than a dish, more than a meal. It's a way of life.'

The dish, he later explained as we sat in the now-impeccable dining room of his restaurant, is the embodiment of this land, of the ingredients it produces and of the lives of locals whose values reach back through the centuries. Garcia was a chef alright, but as I listened to him, I realized he was also a fabulous storyteller, a philosopher perhaps. He promised he would show me some of his poems, thought I might enjoy the one about the bouquet garni. Who was this man?

'One hears there are as many recipes for cassoulet as there are cooks,' he said later, 'but let's start at the source,' and he pointed to the 1938 edition of the *Larousse Gastronomique* on a shelf in his sunny kitchen. Julia Child, who dedicated six pages to cassoulet in her seminal treatise *Mastering the Art of French Cooking*, once wrote that if she were allowed only one reference book in her library, *Larousse Gastronomique* would be it, 'without question'.

'Look at page 297,' he said, handing me the *Larousse*. 'The article on cassoulet starts with a recipe written as a poem.' He recited the whole thing by heart. This was not the hymn I had been fortunate enough to hear the day before, but it sounded like a love song celebrating the local province and the deliciousness of the dish. '*So good you'll want to lick your fingers.*'

He was sitting, but he didn't fully occupy his chair. He kept one leg tucked under the table while the other jetted straight towards the kitchen. In time, I learned that this old-school cook barely ever sat, and that on the rare occasion he did, he kept jumping up to check the stove. And that he believed his constant searing knee pain was just part of the métier.

He flipped the book open. 'Here's author Anatole France's favorite cassoulet from Chez Clémence on Rue Vavin in Paris,' said Garcia, referring to the winner of the 1921 Nobel Prize in Literature. Suddenly he climbed on the chair.

'From Histoire Comique, 1903!' he announced, and started reading:

'*Let me take you to Chez Clémence, a small bistro that serves only one dish, but an extraordinary one. It's cassoulet from Castelnaudary. Clémence's cassoulet has been simmering for twenty years. She might add goose, sausage or beans from time to time, but the core is the same. And this ancient, treasured core exudes the same flavor one finds in the amber-toned women of the old Venetian's Masters.*'

He got down, wiping his eyes. I clapped, but I was stunned.

Weren't we here to discuss cuisine? I felt I was getting a course in literature – or was it art history?

'But the recipe, chef?'

He sat again and sighed.

'Some say there are as many recipes as there are cooks,' he said, 'but that's not true.' He pointed to a small yellow book on the table. 'This is *The Occitan Feast*, written by Montagné in 1929.' He paused, and then whispered, 'Sylvie, there are *only* three recipes.'

I read, '*Cassoulet is the God of the Occitan cuisine. The version from Castelnaudary is God the Father, the Carcassonne recipe is God the Son, and the Toulouse one is the Holy Spirit.*'

'Do you understand? There are only three recipes, and each emerged in a different town.' His tone had turned harsh.

In nearby Castelnaudary, the self-proclaimed world capital of cassoulet, he said with a sneer, fresh pork, ham, shank, sausage, and pork skin get added to the beans. In Carcassonne, it's red partridge when you can hunt, or duck confit and pork, and in Toulouse, cooks start with the Castelnaudary version and add pork belly, mutton neck or breast, as well as goose or duck confit. The whole thing should have signaled indigestion, but I was getting hungry just listening to him.

Garcia told me that legend had the dish originating during the Hundred Years War (1337–1453), the longest and perhaps worst conflicts that opposed 'Frogs' (the name the English gave the French) and 'Roastbif' (the French always derided the English taste for overcooked meat).

Outside the French town of Castelnaudary, in the heart of the old Occitan region, he continued, while the English army was preparing for what it hoped would be the final assault, the besieged town's provost called for a banquet to hearten the population and asked that every citizen bring out any food left. White beans, herbs, and chunks of meat – pork, lamb, goose, sausages – were thrown into one massive pot and cooked together over the coals. As the story goes, empowered by the cassoulet they had just invented, a loaded army of Frogs rushed at the Roastbif assailants, driving them all the way back to the beaches of Normandy (about 500 miles).

Listening to Garcia was exhausting. He seemed to take on every role in the story and was out of breath by the time he was done. But I wanted more. I'd never met someone with that kind of aura. He drew me in.

'*Papa, tu viens?*' The voice came from the kitchen. It was Guy, Garcia's only son and designated heir. Tall, dark, and wiry, he wore his Iberian heritage on his apron.

'Later,' said the chef as he disappeared into the kitchen.

'More coffee?' asked a sweet voice.

I jumped. Laurence, Garcia's wife, a diminutive woman, wore a white turtleneck, thin glasses, and slippers which allowed her to glide on the red ceramic tiles.

'Yes, thank you,' I said. 'Laurence, can you sit with me for a bit?' I asked. 'I am confused. I came to write an article about a dish and now I find out there's a whole world in it.'

She sat, almost reluctantly, as if she didn't know how to stop working. Born only a few miles away from the Cité, she reminisced about her grandmother, clad in black, picking the broken beans from the bucket and swearing in Occitan under her breath every time she found one. She would soak them on Friday evenings, prepare the stew on Saturdays and drop it at the village baker on Sundays so he could bake it in his massive wood-burning oven while the family went to mass.

'Each woman from the village carried her cassoulet in a *cassole*, made with red earth from the village of Issel,' she said. 'They all met at the baker's oven, supposedly for the cassoulet, but it was all about the village's gossip.'

What a different world I came from. On Friday nights, my paternal grandmother lit the Shabbat candles in her gilded dining room while the staff waited in the antechamber until she'd press the bell hidden under the carpet.

'You have to understand,' said Laurence, 'cassoulet is what keeps us together.'

What kept my family together? I wondered.

7

Carcassonne, April 2008

ON MY THIRD AND LAST DAY IN CARCASSONNE, THE RUSH
of a newspaper slipping under my door woke me. A bit unsteady –
that Minervois wine hadn't seemed that potent, but how many glasses
had I downed? – I struggled to remember exactly why I was here,
but slid out of bed to pick up the paper. I opened it and, instantly,
I knew. On the front page of today's *Midi Libre* was a long article
about last night's raid in Les Halles, the bountiful covered market
a few steps away. The thieves fled, the report said, with duck and
pork sausages, four large hams, six foies gras and a few *entrecôte*s.
This, in delicious Carcassonne, was front-page news.

It was early, and the hordes of day-trippers hadn't crossed the
drawbridge yet. But in the town kitchens, aromatic herbs and diced
vegetables conspired all night to infuse the broth that now boiled away
in gigantic stainless-steel vats. In the mornings, Carcassonne smelled

like cassoulet. My nose started twitching and I was instantly hungry, but there was no time. Garcia had agreed to continue working on my education, this time about the *cassole*: the magnificent terracotta vessel that wraps itself around the stew and, after hours in the oven, brings it to heavenly crustiness.

'There are many contradictory theories about which bowl to use,' the chef had declared. 'I'll take you to the Vat factory along the canal. Perhaps you'll get why they're wrong and I'm right.'

At the bottom of the fortress, Garcia was already waiting for me in the old Renault. I knew he now respected me a little, because he kissed me four times on the cheeks – a regional and generous tradition that ensures everyone always passes the various microbes of the season back and forth. The car smelled of fresh blood and thyme.

'Next time I'll have to take you to the Montagne Noire for the wild herbs,' he said suddenly. He didn't say more, but I smiled. Somehow, I'd passed the test: we both knew I was coming back.

As soon as we left the outskirts of town, I felt I had jumped into one of Mary Poppins's chalk drawings. A mosaic of undulating fields in bloom spilled on all sides of the car. It was only April, but we were not far from the Mediterranean Sea and the landscape was already trying on its summer wardrobe.

We crossed a small stone bridge over the canal, still and timeless, then pulled over in front of a low stone building inscribed '1830'. Its roof was layered with red bricks encircling a very tall chimney. We got out of the car and started walking towards the entrance when a short, stocky man came out in a fury.

'You, Garcia, back off,' he yelled.

'But I called, I brought a journalist from—'

'Back off, I said. How can you dare come here! Go away!'

Still entranced by the serenity of the landscape, I suddenly found myself in the middle of what felt like a boxing ring. More men came out and they stood still in their muddy aprons, their arms crossed. They looked like dirty butchers, and I had no intention of being made into sausage. No one spoke as I turned to Garcia.

'Last month,' he explained, 'I finally told the truth about their *cassoles* to the local newspaper.'

'What truth?' I asked, my eye on the mob.

'They call the *grésales cassoles*,' he said darkly, as if that declaration explained why I was standing in the middle of southwestern France, probably about to be murdered.

I couldn't understand what was being said next, because the men reverted to speaking Occitan. By then they were yelling what couldn't possibly be niceties, but Garcia pointed to me and pushed me forward.

'I told them you were an American journalist, so they're going to show you the factory, but don't tell them you speak French. Go, go,' he whispered, shoving me towards the butchers.

'But what about you?'

'They won't let me in,' he muttered, shrugging his wide shoulders.

I took a few steps and then, mustering my courage, extended my hand.

'Bonjour,' the mustachioed potter said, not taking my hand.

I followed him inside, feeling queasy, wondering if I would ever see the light of day again. As soon as I entered the potters' lair, I plunged into the underworld. It was hard to breathe and the air, thick with reddish earth powder, made me cough. I heard a strange cacophony, as if an entire percussion section were rehearsing madly.

'We work the way our ancestors worked a hundred years ago,' said my handler, who turned out to be one of the Vat brothers, the fifth-generation owners. 'There's been no progress made in our field,' he continued, 'because there's no need to do anything differently.'

The men were back at work. Now I could see that some of them were actually quite young, but the physical work had taken its toll. Perhaps it was also that damn dust. I watched the way they sat, low, their arms outstretched as if embracing the wheels. Crumbs of clay flew around as their feet pushed the wheel underneath, willing it to whirl faster and faster. The clay landed on their aprons but also on their clothes, their shoes, their hair, their skin. At first, the hands cradled a magma of living clay and barely moved. But as I approached, I saw the fingers caressing, cuddling, pleating the clay as if it were silk. And out of that mass, a bowl suddenly rose, seemingly on its own and magically becoming wider at the top. The hands were dancing now, and I wondered how they would feel on my skin. I couldn't reckon that they belonged to these 'butchers'.

'Father didn't ask us if we were interested in pottery,' said Vat. 'There was work to be done and I wasn't good in school. I had to make myself useful. It was 1964,' he added. 'I was fourteen.'

And it was the same for his son, André. 'I was partying a bit too much, so I was told to come to the factory, first on my days off from school, then every day.' He had been there since 1985.

Garcia had told me that the only proper clay for *cassoles* came from Issel, a village only a few miles away, and that the Vat brothers had a quarry there. 'We do it all, from extracting the clay to selling the pots, the pitchers, the bowls.'

As I moved into another room, leaving traces of mud behind me, I finally understood where the constant banging came from. Near the massive wood-burning oven, filled to the brim with rows and rows of conical bowls, the men banged metal rods against them as they were taken out. They were testing the clay to make sure it was sturdy enough to withstand a lifetime of cassoulet-making.

'How many of them break when they first come out?' I asked.

'Since 1964, I've seen perhaps two?' said the potter.

I didn't dare ask about Garcia while in the factory, but as soon as I was let out, I strode to his car.

'So, what's the story with the *cassoles*?' I asked.

His fury returned instantly.

'The shelves in their oven are configured in such a way that they can bake more bowls if they make conical ones, but these are not *cassoles*. It's criminal; it's slander! What they call *cassoles* are in fact *grésales*, the containers with a spout my grandparents used to rinse the salt out of the cured pork.' He was fuming. I didn't dare ask more as we drove away.

'At home, I have a copy of an article written in 1850 by a writer from Toulouse,' he seethed, 'who describes the *cassole* as "a round, paunchy bowl, with a flat ass". I'll show you.'

Garcia had found an old photograph of a similar bowl and asked a potter friend to replicate the shape. Since then, members of the Academy were required to use the paunchy bowls only.

The chef did not believe in shortcuts. He didn't believe in fudging. Everything he made had to be done 'the right way', even if that took three days. He didn't need bakeries; he cajoled his own *levain*; he woke up at dawn to make stock and would probably throw up if he ever consumed bouillon cube. And no amount of money could ever convince him that cassoulet should be made in a *grésale*, just because their shape fit inside a kiln more easily, meaning that more containers could be made at the same time.

That a local family whose purpose for generations had been to create *cassoles* could change the original shape of the bowl for mercantile reasons was too much for him to bear. In this seemingly simple issue, he recognized everything that was wrong with the modern world, and saw his role as the defender of timeless values and traditions. The battle of the paunchy bowl with the flat ass against the conical container with the spout was both universal and crucial.

Around what I assumed was a simple stew, it seemed I'd uncovered enough battles to write several operas.

8

New York, spring 2008

I KISSED ALL THE GARCIAS GOODBYE FOUR TIMES AND retraced my steps towards New York City, eyes and palate still dreaming of cassoulet. At the airport, my husband was waiting for me with a sign that said, 'Sylvie Bigar, Travel Writer'. It was such a sweet gesture. Kennedy International Airport is only sixteen miles from Manhattan, where we lived, but the road is so congested it can take an hour and a half or more to get there. I was very touched, but tension set in as soon as we got in the car. Staying home with the children while managing an all-encompassing career had been stressful. I thanked him and tried to show how grateful I was, but I wondered silently how my career would affect our relationship.

As we crossed the Triboro Bridge on the way home from the airport, I watched the skyline of my life appear like a mirage. What was real? The land of the ancestral stew or the futuristic urban lot

I had called home for the last two decades? I was thrilled to see my children again and made a point over the next few weeks to be present with them, physically and emotionally. Back in my routine, I craved straightforward ingredients, as if in need of a cleanse. I ate a lot of green salads and sashimi.

Incapable of making sense of the deep feelings I harbored, I wrote a simple story about the legends and the facts surrounding the history of cassoulet. I sensed that under the discovery of this dish and my intense emotional reaction, there were ramifications to explore. But where to start? And why? It was a mystery.

A few months later, I received a call from another magazine editor who had read my piece and thought it would be interesting to compare and contrast the various clay pots used in the cassoulet process. Soon I was peering over my notes again, reliving the battle of the *cassoles*. In my mind, I heard Garcia's voice, his desperate tone as he recounted the way young chefs were not trained well, ignored the old books, let the bottom line rule rather than the stove. I knew he belonged to a dying breed and that I could learn so much from him – not only about food, it seemed, but also about a certain way of life, some nebulous quality of living that I was craving and that was missing from my American lifestyle.

A month later, I heard that Lyon had become a cradle for young creative chefs. At the beginning of the twentieth century, a food critic named Curnonsky had dubbed the town 'World Capital of Gastronomy', but past visits had yielded sad saucissons and catatonic quenelles. Now, it seemed, things were changing. Intrigued, a magazine editor offered to send me to investigate; I jumped at the opportunity to leave home again.

My paternal grandmother Madeleine was born in Lyon, and throughout my childhood my father kept an office there, two hours away by car. He would go every Thursday and bring back the same fluid *fromage blanc en faisselle*, one of Lyon's specialties, which my three sisters and I would lap slowly, arguing endlessly over whether it was better with or without sugar. The Lyon I returned to had cleaned up nicely, shedding its provincial veil of grit and crime and acquiring a polished persona. I strolled through Renaissance-era quarters, soaking in their soft coral glow, and peeked into age-old artisanal ateliers.

Everywhere I went, people were eating. The old *bouchons* (the Lyonnais relative of the Parisian bistro) still served cornichons in tall earthenware jars with worn-out wooden tongs clipped to their thick love handles, but young chefs were popping up all over town. The hippest bistro was called Le Bouchon des Filles and, downtown, Nicolas Le Bec, a blond and tousled enfant terrible who wore black in the kitchen, had garnered two Michelin stars for his eponymous restaurant. He had subsequently launched a sleek casual eatery at the airport, and now ran a whole culinary complex in the new Confluence area. Gourmands whispered that he was the new Bocuse.

Paul Bocuse, eighty-three, was still going strong. Since 1965 he had held on to the meaningful trio of Michelin stars – the top marks on the French gastronomy ladder – for his rigorous take on simple regional cuisine. A brilliant communicator with a fierce dedication to local fresh ingredients, he was also the very first celebrity chef, with a *Time* magazine cover. Fellow Lyonnais Daniel Boulud, with whom I would end up writing a cookbook a few years later, spent some time in Bocuse's kitchen as a teenager and once described him as 'a French national treasure'. For chef Alain Ducasse, he was the 'pope of French cuisine', even though it was a public 'secret' that this particular pope shared his life with not two but three ladies!

The morning of my arrival, I phoned Martine, Bocuse's cousin, who worked as his assistant. 'Come at eleven,' she ordered in an efficient high pitch, directing me to arrive at L'Auberge du Pont de Collonges, the three-Michelin-star gastronomic hothouse established by Bocuse's grandparents on the banks of the river Saône. In addition to this flagship, Bocuse had opened five brasseries, as well as a fast-food joint in Lyon, aided by his right-hand man, Jean Fleury, a burly and solid businessman with a powerful French nose.

This empire building, French style, had begun early. As a young boy in the 1940s Bocuse apprenticed with la Mère Brazier, one of the first cooks who helped write the Lyonnais tradition of great, simple cuisine, and the first woman to receive three stars from the Michelin Guide. He followed with eight years at La Pyramide under the genial Fernand Point, a joyous and generous giant for whom the third Michelin star had literally been invented.

'Collonges,' I told the grumpy driver of the taxi I hailed in the center of Lyon.

'But he's not open for lunch,' he responded, turning around to see who could possibly not know that. Just as in Carcassonne, I felt that the world of food was completely woven into the fabric of society. Michelin-starred chefs did not exist in a rarefied world dedicated to higher echelons or rich foreigners. This taxi driver then went on to describe every minute of the meal he'd had there, twenty-three years ago, for his mother-in-law's sixtieth birthday. He, just like Garcia, was proud of Bocuse, proud of the land that had nourished such a chef and proud he had been able to partake in the feast.

Bright green with red shutters lined with orange, the garish colors of the *auberge* surprised me, but their boldness made me smile. Nearby, colorful frescoes (that green and orange palette again) relayed the history of gastronomy, starting with an ode to Marie-Antonin Carême – the first cook to codify French cuisine during the Napoleonic Era – and a tableau featuring Fernand and Mado Point.

Flapping proudly over the restaurant, the American flag paid tribute to the Normandy saviors, reminding me that Lyon was a stronghold of the French Resistance and that American soldiers had taken excellent care of a wounded eighteen-year-old Bocuse, who was freshly enlisted.

'Sylvie?'

Fashionably clad in black slacks and a polo shirt, the chef whom everyone called Monsieur Paul was ready for our interview. Ever so charming, he asked about my life in New York. The words flew. I was struck by the difference between his poise and networking skills and Garcia's inner rage. Monsieur Paul was a consummate diplomat who'd invented the persona of the celebrity chef, out in the dining room schmoozing with clients and journalists. He traveled the world promoting a polished and fanciful image of the French chef. Garcia, by contrast, lived and breathed at the stove. His hands showed burns, cuts, and a lifetime spent cooking for others.

I steered the conversation back to the kitchen.

'If you start with great ingredients, you have great cuisine,' Monsieur Paul explained. 'We the cooks don't decide much, the clients do.' Trends? 'It's just like in fashion. One year it's the miniskirt, another it's the maxi. Me?' He'd exploded with laughter. 'I like all skirts!'

At the end of our conversation, Bocuse stood up abruptly. 'You're having dinner here tonight, and bring a friend.' I didn't think to argue, or to tell him that I was supposed to be on a train to Paris for the evening flight to New York. Nothing else mattered. I would be having dinner at Paul Bocuse that night. Back home in New York, my kids wouldn't understand, and my husband would tense his jaw and pretend he did. It wasn't like I was cheating on him with Bocuse.

That night, my Lyonnais friend Blandine, a fellow gourmande, and I giggled like two schoolgirls as we approached the restaurant in the pouring rain. I had not known Blandine long, but the way she closed her eyes while tasting a bite of foie gras convinced me she was the perfect accomplice. Monsieur Paul, supremely elegant in his starched whites, kissed each of us on both cheeks and led us to a round table in the corner, assuredly putting us under the intense spell of the chef in the tall toque.

The classic decor, with its crystal chandeliers, antique mirrors, rustic furniture, and heavy curtains shone under a thousand lights. The atmosphere was bubbly. Diners were elated to be there, ready for the experience of a lifetime. Some had waited months to get a reservation. We all craned our necks to see what the next table was being served by the perfect black-and-white ballet of elegant waiters carrying twinkling silver trays and steamy copper pans.

We started with the famous *soupe aux truffes noires V.G.E.*, a truly presidential appetizer that Bocuse created in 1975 for then French President Valéry Giscard d'Estaing. The dish was served to him at the luncheon that followed Bocuse's nomination as *Chevalier de la Légion d'Honneur*.

Preceded by a whiff of truffle, a puffy golden hot air balloon anchored to a ceramic soup tureen floated my way. I pierced the crust and plunged in my spoon. The combination of truffles and foie gras was not innovative, but the intensity of the broth added the essential ingredient – pleasure. As we proceeded with the *filet de sole aux nouilles Fernand Point* – resembling a fish gratin – and then a *pigeon en feuilleté au chou nouveau*, it dawned on me that dining at Bocuse was about much more than delicious food. It was a temple dedicated to the fine dining of another era.

The cheese shop where my father had bought his fromage blanc, la Mère Brazier, and Fernand Point were long gone. But seated in Bocuse's timeless dining room, with the thick tablecloth under my fingers, savoring the classic dishes I had only read about in culinary anthologies, I could taste the past. It was a completely different experience than Carcassonne, but the restaurant and his cuisine felt like a time capsule, and an important lesson to experience in my personal culinary journey.

৵৵

Back in New York, there was plenty to keep me busy. My children were seven and five, and Chocolat, our sweet mutt, was eight. I had chosen to enroll the children in a demanding French school, and they were struggling. My husband and I spoke English to each other, and I would switch to French every time I addressed them. Passing on the language and, I hoped, the culture of France was crucial to me, but the school placed high demands on us. There were reunions, planning committees, volunteer obligations. I felt pulled in myriad directions, trying to fulfill my deadlines and find time to research and dream up new stories.

But after the 2008 crash of the market, numerous editors lost their jobs and the work dried up. I embarked on a project to write a book about a floral designer friend from Provence and spent months struggling to remember the names of flowers we were describing and photographing. I couldn't wait to get back to the world of food and travel.

By 2009 I was on the road again, to Prague, to write about young chefs rediscovering the Austro-Hungarian culinary traditions, and to Morocco to meet the seventeen women, each one responsible for a different dish, who made up the brigade at the Moroccan restaurant La Mamounia in Marrakech.

When the weather turned cold again in the fall, I tried to ignore the stirrings in my belly. I wasn't hungry for fried chicken or ribs.

Instead, I caught myself revisiting the various steps in the process of making cassoulet, trying to put it all to rest.

But I couldn't. And the more I thought about this dish and this region, the more I was intrigued – obsessed, really. I googled cassoulet and found hundreds of recipes, then I stumbled on a French hidden camera episode depicting a scene at a market in Castelnaudary. A British actor set up a stall touting the merits of the 'English cassoulet', and hailing local shoppers, trying to convince them that the real cassoulet had been invented in the UK. It started with laughs, but the atmosphere soon turned tense, then dramatic, and the actor almost got hurt. A dish worth battling for? A dish people felt passionate about? I'd always followed my passions – would I find my own gourmand Camelot if I dug under the crust?

Finally, in the dead of winter, while the children were napping, I mustered the courage to call Garcia.

'Eric, it's Sylvie.'

'Sylvie who?'

That hurt.

'Oh, come on,' I tried to keep it light, 'you know that many Sylvies?'

'Bonjour, what's up?' he asked, neutral.

'I want to come back and learn to make it.'

'Why?'

'I am not sure why, chef, but it's been more than a year and I still think about it.'

'Do they feed you enough over there, in America?'

I laughed.

'I want to come back and apprentice with you. Maybe if I learn to cook a cassoulet, I'll be able to make one every time I crave it, and then I'll be able to move on.'

'*D'accord*,' he said, sneering, and hung up.

9

Geneva, 1970s

I GREW UP JEWISH. AND IN THE CALVINIST GENEVA OF THE 1960s and 70s, that was quite exotic.

'What did you get for Christmas?' my peers would ask at the International School of Geneva, where I remained, throughout ten years of schooling, the only Jew in my class.

'What do you mean, you don't celebrate Christmas?'

My mother was born in Paris in 1925 to serious agnostics whose personal calendar was French and secular. What that meant was that the year was articulated around the *grandes vacances*, the summer vacation they spent in Brittany on the Western Coast of France one year and in the Alps, where the whole family enjoyed hiking and even alpinism, the next. *Hue, la grosse!* 'Move along, fatty,' my grandfather would tell my mother, mocking her chubby body as she tottered behind him along the Alpine paths.

As a child in the Paris of the 1930s, she enjoyed the family's simple Christmas tree, as well as her mother's *dinde aux marrons*, the traditionally French turkey with chestnuts. At Easter, my mother, Anne, and her brother, Frédéric, painted the eggs their parents would hide in the Jardin du Ranelagh near their apartment.

'I'd never even heard of Yom Kippur,' she'd tell me. This felt odd, since her own great-grandfather had worked as a rabbi in Alsace. 'When my father spoke of his grandfather,' she'd say, 'he was a bit ironic, a bit condescending.' Decades later, I would find letters from the rabbi, exhorting his children and grandchildren to keep kosher, to go to shul, to safeguard their heritage, but his wishes went unanswered. A few years before World War II, my maternal grandparents, Daniel and Iris Kaufman, didn't think of themselves as Jews.

My father's childhood at the mansion set on Rue Saint-Victor near the old town of Geneva was anything but simple. The third floor was the domain of a Swiss German nanny named Nana and the children, Frédéric, who would become my father, and his older sister Rose. Nana ran a tight ship. 'She was strict and mean, I hated her,' my father would say, decades later. I'd never heard him speak this harshly about anyone.

The Rue Saint-Victor Christmas tree was gigantic, extravagant. It was set in the middle of the living room for all to admire. The family exchanged gifts at Christmas and toasted the new year on January first, not on Rosh Hashanah.

My mother would have allowed it but, strangely, my father was adamant we couldn't have a Christmas tree, so I grew up with a bad case of tree envy. If my parents went out during the holidays, I would hide behind the flowery curtains and watch the Citroën leave its nervous scratch on our graveled courtyard, and then I'd dash out of my girly bedroom and slide down the wooden banister, jump down and run to the small, dark dining room where the staff ate their meals. There, in the corner, hid the Christmas tree Joachim and his wife Carmela, our cook, dressed up every year with all the shiny ornaments they'd brought from Spain. I inhaled its woodsy alpine smell, touched the pink and purple tinsel that circled its girth and the multicolored baubles that hung from every branch, reminiscent of an old gypsy's dangling earrings. I can still see the glittering white star at the tip of the tree, the shining beacon of my long-gone childhood.

At school, I hated feeling different, but I enjoyed the traditions we followed at home: one gift for each of the eight nights of Hanukkah, the winter festival of lights; the pure pleasure of wedging my tongue through the salted butter and thick honey I ladled on a matzoh cracker (the unleavened bread eaten at Passover); heading to synagogue to hear the deep baritone of the young rabbi on Friday nights.

Sometime in the 60s, my adventurous parents left my sisters and me with our maternal grandparents and flew with a group of friends to New York City, where they proceeded to buy a used 1960 Buick station wagon. The plan was to cross the United States and end up in San Francisco, where we had cousins. They had decided to take their time and take the southern route. One Friday night, the group found itself in Dallas, Texas.

'Why don't we try to find a synagogue?' one of them asked, which is how five Swiss citizens ended up in a reform congregation in the middle of a Dallas suburb.

'The shock for us was twofold,' my father recounted. 'First, men and women together, meaning families were not split up, and then the service was mostly in English. For the first time, I understood the meaning of the prayers.'

Afterwards, several people approached the small group, introduced themselves, and asked them where they were from.

A lively discussion followed, and the travelers were invited to dinner at the home of the congregation's president. My parents rarely went to synagogue in Geneva, mostly because the average age of the congregants was about eighty. The Friday night service seldom rallied the ten men needed (women were not counted within that traditionalist group), and the Hebrew-only prayers didn't appeal. It would take years, but upon their return my parents started the process that would launch the first French-speaking Reform congregation in Switzerland. Its very first Friday night service took place in our home, in the library. I was seven.

Our family was more attached to the cultural traditions than the religious rites, but *bien sûr* we never ate pork. That is, except *jambon de Paris* (Parisian ham), but my mother assured me that didn't really count.

And it was this convoluted culinary contradiction that hit me one day. I must have been eight or so. I knew ham was pork. Grown-ups lied. That gave me pause. A narrow fissure opened in my psyche and something I now recognize as anxiety poured in. Things were not always what they seemed to be.

On both sides, our heritage was clearly Ashkenazi with seemingly straightforward Eastern European roots. In terms of genealogy, all roads led to the region of Alsace in the north of France, famous for *choucroute*, the pork orgy served over sauerkraut that my blond, blue-eyed maternal grandfather adored. There, in a town called Colmar, many Adlers, I had been told, lay in the Jewish cemetery. A cousin had tracked down relatives living in the area as early as 1690. Before that, Jews were not inscribed in the local city archives. And before Alsace? Probably Poland, I'd been told, vaguely.

Discreetly, my parents looked down on Sephardic Jews. The melodies they sang at services resembled Arabic chanting, their food was oily, and they were unsophisticated.

But what about my father's tanned complexion? He was often thought to be from Spain or the Middle East. His reputation as an accomplished sailor was at its peak in the mid-1970s, but when someone called on behalf of Baron Marcel Bich, the billionaire of the Bic disposable pen and razor empire, we thought it was a joke. It wasn't. Would my father be interested in helping train the French team that would challenge the America's Cup a year later? Of course he would! Baron Bich, a self-made Italian-born entrepreneur, by then a naturalized French national, was obsessed with the America's Cup and would spend millions on boats and people in his effort to win the elusive prize.

And so it was that most summer weekends, my father and his two sailing acolytes would be plucked by private jet and brought to the Bay of Quiberon in Brittany, the French region on the Atlantic Ocean. There, my father steered the magnificent twelve-meter *Constellation* against the Baron's hopeful *France*. One time, on his way out, he asked my mother what he could bring her back. Lobsters, she joked.

This was Switzerland, the landlocked country of Heidi, so lobsters rarely appeared on menus, but that Sunday night my father came home with a large paper bag in which four Breton blue lobsters were fighting for their freedom. I can still hear the terrible sound of their claws and legs raking against the paper. He promptly released them on the marble floor of the monumental hallway, to our stupefaction and horror. They attempted to crawl away, but destiny awaited. They were promptly dunked in an upstairs bathtub and later cooked by Carmela. I could not fathom eating creatures I had seen alive, but the adults had a banquet. The word 'treif', non-kosher, was never uttered.

Strangely, I felt close to the Sephardic world. I loved the warmth and expansive personalities of my Sephardic friends. And there was my son's skin, the color of poured caramel; in Italy, people always thought I was Italian; when I explored Andalusia in the South of Spain, locals addressed me in Spanish, and when I discovered Essaouira on the Atlantic Coast of Morocco, I almost bought a riad and dreamt of moving there permanently.

'*Tu es marocaine*?' shopkeepers would ask me.

I never had any desire to see Poland. Recently, a friend told me about her interest in the Jews' forced migration from Spain after the Inquisition in 1534.

'Are you aware,' she asked, 'that hundreds of thousands of them somehow made their way from Spain to Alsace in Northern France?'

'No,' I uttered, 'I didn't know.'

Was that it?

Was part of me Sephardic? That would certainly explain my father's looks and my Mediterranean temperament! Because Spain abutted France, it was easy to extrapolate. Had my ancestors been kicked out of Spain? Had they stopped in the southwest of France on their way to Alsace? Had they savored cassoulet? Were there ancestral beans running through my veins?

10

Carcassonne, March 2010

'YOU HAVEN'T STARTED YET?'

Garcia, a tad grayer than when I last saw him two years earlier, strode into the bright kitchen with the assurance of a toreador, his eye on the pig's head.

'Bonjour, chef, how are you?' I asked in my most chirpy tone.

'Bonjour, let's get to work.'

The fact that I might need a shower or perhaps to change was of no concern to the chef, so I washed my hands, slipped my apron on and picked up the knife.

I was scared. I had never held anything that sharp, so I positioned myself on the other side of the counter and tried to copy Garcia. First, we removed the pointy ears, cutting the elastic membrane in ribbons and then into pieces the size of stamps. Which sounds would this pig have heard in its young life? The incessant chatter of siblings in the pen? Mice scurrying in the hay? Birds outside?

Our knives dug deeper along the skull, his flowing through, mine hitting bone and cartilage as we scooped through the cheeks. I fought two opposing currents. On one hand, I was glad to face what it meant to eat meat, to use a weapon to transform a living being into a dish, but on the other, I was horrified. There was an acrid smell and even though all the blood had been drained out, nothing had prepared me for this. Not the hours spent watching Carmela in the kitchen of my youth, not my feeble attempts at cooking for my family, and not the time I had spent in professional restaurants, safely sheltered behind my notebook, jotting thoughts for recipes or chef profiles. What I had discovered, though, when I briefly worked as a recipe tester for a famous food writer, was that I could count on my palate. I instinctively knew the zucchini needed more salt to bloom, that another glug of olive oil in the smashed potatoes with rosemary would quench their thirst and smooth their flesh, how less sugar would allow a chocolate mousse to breathe and shine. But I'd never cooked in a restaurant kitchen. I'd never broken an animal down.

I tried very hard not to stare at its snout, at its teeth. After a while, the chef took over and, with the precision of a surgeon, he cut away any semblance of life.

I had had very little experience with death, and none with dead heads. When we put the mountain of pig in the fridge, I finally relaxed and started breathing normally again. I looked around. This had to be the nicest kitchen I'd ever seen. Most restaurant kitchens in cities are hidden in basements, with no windows or access to fresh air. Couple that with professional stoves and grills and you tend to find yourself in fiery hell. At Domaine Balthazar, ancient wooden window frames held row after row of glass panes that opened onto the day. Just outside, roses climbed up the cracked walls and, now that the beast was gone, I could detect their faint scent. The gleaming surface of the counters was scrubbed constantly – by the end of my *stage*, I would become a scrubbing pro – and the walls of white tiles reflected their light. Smack in the middle sat an ancient stove that looked strangely like a Volkswagen Beetle.

'This ol' stove works better than any modern I've seen,' said Garcia proudly.

Next, the chef showed me a bag of onions, the size of a young child.

'Peel,' he ordered. 'Onions are the foundations of the kitchen.' And he disappeared outside.

I obeyed and, taking a bigger knife, went to town, but the second I cut into the first bulb, my eyes started to well up. And that was probably all I needed to burst into tears. Alone among steaming pots and a river of onions, I cried. I cried because I wasn't good at peeling onions. I cried for the pig. I cried for my father, who had died a few years earlier, three weeks before my son was born. I cried for my childhood and my youth now gone too.

'What's going on?' asked Laurence, who appeared next to me in her slippers, as quiet as ever.

'Nothing, sorry, I am a bit tired,' I responded.

'Come on, you need to rest.'

I slept ten hours. When I woke up, in my simple room above the restaurant, it was morning and I was starving. I got dressed and came down barefoot, my feet caressing the rugged stone steps. Not a sound could be heard as I stepped into the dining room, but there they all were, having breakfast.

'Slept well?' asked Laurence. Even though it was July, she was wearing a long-sleeve polo shirt buttoned all the way up. She was sipping tea. Guy and his wife Sabine waved at me while their youngest son Pascal's four-year-old face disappeared behind the crock he gripped with his pudgy hands.

'Put the bowl down and say good morning,' growled Garcia, even though he hadn't greeted me. Reluctantly, the child obeyed.

'Bonjour, madame.'

'Bonjour, Pascal!' I said, admiring the thickness of the rustic bowl. Then I saw it was a small earthenware *cassole*, and realized the child had been slurping cassoulet for breakfast.

11

Carcassonne, March 2010

I DIDN'T EAT CASSOULET FOR BREAKFAST THAT FIRST morning at the Garcias' in Carcassonne, and I didn't sip red wine, even though they all did. Yes, the kids too. The dish played a crucial role in the family's diet. Or perhaps it was more than their diet. The chef made cassoulet three times a week and there was always some left over and that was that. It would sustain, it would support. In the Aude, one of the poorest French *départements*, food was no entertainment. Food was life.

I had *café au lait* and a thick *tartine*, a hefty slice of peasant bread Laurence cut for me. Creamy, yellow butter made it scrumptious. For once, Garcia stayed at the table. He'd seemed gruff on the phone when I had called from New York, but it was this very morning that I first felt he was intrigued by my obsession and, dare I say it, touched that I was back to learn more. Had the pig's head been a test of my resolve?

'It's one thing to master a dish,' he said softly, 'it's another to understand where it comes from, how it travels from the bounties of the regional soil and into the kitchen. I know you're itching to get your hands dirty, but I think you literally need to get your feet in our dirt first.'

I was instructed to stand at the counter, my hands thrust deep into an immense bucket, and pick through what looked like a stream of white beans, the size of beads, to remove any that were broken or stained. They felt soft, almost like an immense rosary. I thought I'd be done quickly, but it took more than two hours. Every time I called him over to announce I was done, he'd find more I'd missed. My legs were hurting, but I held on: how many hours could I stand like that without moving? Finally, he asked me to step away and poured the beans into a massive pot filled with water and fresh bay leaves and left them to soak.

Back in the car, no smell of blood this time, we headed towards the hills on our way to the duck farm. I had traveled through France extensively. Geneva lies only four or five hours north of Provence, so for school vacations, my family would often drive south on the iconic Nationale 7, the ancient Roman way that connects Paris to Menton near Nice, through lavender fields and rows of cypress with elongated limbs, but the Aude landscape was completely different. Garcia and I rode first through lush forests of chestnut trees and venerable oaks – 'Where elk and boars roam,' he said, 'but you'll never see them' – and then alongside dramatic, rocky peaks crowned by ruins of Cathar outposts and castles. The Cathars were a religious group that emerged in the early Middle Ages and flourished in the Languedoc until the Catholic Church, invoking heresy, called for a deadly Crusade against them.

We turned into a small lane and got out in front of a stone house with wooden doors. On each one, the naïf profile of a duck had been carved, and above the door, a stone duck heralded the entrance. There was no mistaking where we were.

'Ducks were domesticated since Roman times,' explained the farmer, Patrick Lauzy, as we toured the farm, 'and duck confit is a crucial part of cassoulet.'

To make duck confit, a cook salts a piece of duck, usually the leg, and lets it rest overnight or longer to drain the moisture out before cooking it in its own fat. The leg is then preserved in yet more fat in a glass jar. This may sound utterly disgusting, even inedible to some, but it is both delicious and even healthy (more on fat later). Throughout the southwest of France, the best chunks of pork, goose, rabbits and game are confit and installed into prized cans and glass jars – a far cry from spam!

It had started to rain as we left the house and walked towards the forest, the path quickly flowing into mud.

'You need boots,' said Garcia, as if he couldn't believe I had shown up so unprepared. I acquiesced as Lauzy told the story of the five-generation farm and how the world of duck had changed since he was a child.

'It's the Americans' fault,' said Lauzy.

'What do you mean?' asked Garcia.

'With the foie gras.'

'What about the foie gras?'

'They say it hurts the animals, ha!' said Lauzy. 'Can you imagine?'

'Well, it can't be pleasant,' I said.

Garcia shot me a dark look.

'Anyway, Lauzy,' he said, 'let's not blame the Americans. Without them our foie gras would be *boche*.'

He was using the French derogatory term for Germans that originated during World War II, a word my mother spoke every

time she recounted her flight from the soldiers who had invaded her
beloved country.

'*Je les emmerde les Américains,*' (fuck the Americans) said Lauzy.

Were we going to be thrown out from the duck farm too? But
Garcia started barking in Occitan and I strolled ahead, as if this
debate did not concern me one bit. Soaked and muddy, I approached
the immense fenced-in area where dozens of ducks led their peaceful
lives, blissfully unaware that they would soon be transformed into
carnal delicacies.

I remained silent on the way back, remembering that my father,
who always said he ate to live and didn't live to eat, harbored few
opinions about food. While his parents were notorious bon vivants,
enjoying white wine or champagne with their appetizers, then noted
reds with the meats, and often visiting Michelin-rated restaurants,
my father didn't seem to care what he was served. Then it struck
me: the only dish he ever professed to love was *canard à l'orange*,
an elaborate and ancient recipe of roasted duck cooked with bitter
oranges. How odd for a man who seemed so austere to relish such an
extravagant recipe!

Later, back in the kitchen, Garcia leaned towards me and
whispered, 'In the old days, we didn't use domesticated ducks for
cassoulet. We shot wild partridge.'

I wasn't even sure what a partridge was, besides a kind of wild
bird, but from his secretive attitude it was clear that this piece of
information mattered. One of the first recipes for partridge dates
from 1651, he explained, and was written by François Pierre de la
Varenne. In his early cookbook, *Le Cuisinier François* (The French
Cook), fresh herbs were introduced for the first time, replacing
the exotic spices of the medieval times. 'That's when cooks started
appreciating the flavor of the ingredients.'

Side by side, we cleaned and prepped veal and beef bones, vegetables and a towering bouquet garni. Hours later – days, really – all the simmering, skimming, and praying would create what chefs call 'stock' – the broth that serves as the base for most French sauces, and is crucial in the making of cassoulet.

'There were tons of partridge in the vineyards in the old times,' he continued, 'since they fed on grapes, but they were a bit tough, we had to stew them slowly.' I was only half-listening. Domesticated duck or wild partridge? I was elsewhere, thinking about my father. Who was he really? Domesticated or wild?

12

Geneva, 1970s

DURING MY CHILDHOOD AT BEAU-CHAMP, I WOULD OFTEN
wake up to the rattling sound of the rickety cart Joachim pushed
from the upstairs kitchenette into my parents' bedroom. He'd
prepare their breakfast beverages – a deep, dark, syrupy *café* for my
father and lapsang souchong for my mother – in the main kitchen
on the ground floor, then walk to the staff's dining room, open the
old dumb waiter carved into the wall and slide the two trays inside.
Then he'd pull hard on the thick rope that lifted the contraption up
to the second floor. He would run up the steep staff staircase to collect
the trays and place them on the docile cart. By the time he knocked
on my parents' soundproofed bedroom door, my father would have
finished getting ready in the adjoining bathroom as he listened to the
news on Europe 1, the French radio station. France and the village
of Ferney-Voltaire, where Voltaire, the writer, spent the last twenty

years of his life, stood a mere five minutes from the house, and our family bathed in French civilization and culture. We listened to French radio, watched French television and my parents read mostly French newspapers. We led a French life within the country of Switzerland.

Every morning I knew him, my father ate the same breakfast. I can picture him in his silk pajamas on weekends or wearing his usual suit and tie on weekdays, his knees wedged against the cart, which doubled as a table. He would start by dropping one sugar cube in the Limoges cup. The china was so fine that the hard sugar sounded like a chime. He'd stop, smile at me and drop another. Then he would pour the steamy coffee, unscrew the metallic box of Guigoz milk powder (he was allergic to cow's milk) and add three small scoops. A delicate silver spoon would help mix it all.

Then his elegant hands, always tanned, would unfold the white napkin framed with lace that cradled the three dark slices of toast. Methodically, he would nibble on all three, but not until he'd lifted up the butter knife, spread butter on each one, put the knife down and, using the wooden spoon, dabbed tears of bitter orange jam.

A peck on my mother's lips while she picked at her minuscule breakfast – a ripe peach the color of dawn, perhaps – and he would be off. To the office on weekdays or to sail on many weekends.

I called him Pâ. I do not know how or why the accent circumflex emerged, but it added energy, punch, and authority to a man who didn't need any more. Everyone was afraid of my father. My classmates found him intimidating, my boyfriends whined he was too strict with me, and my sisters feared his scolding tone.

I never did.

My oldest memory of him is a memory of us. It is winter 1967 and we are walking on a beach near Antibes in the South of France, where my grandparents rented a house every winter. All of a sudden, a young man riding a horse bareback emerged out of the haze, walking slowly in the Mediterranean Sea. With every step, the animal broke the surface of the water, creating infinite blue ripples. I don't remember if we spoke, but I remember how my father held my hand tight, how we looked at each other in awe, and the intense happiness we shared at the sight of such beauty. The vision of a young man on his horse, '*le cheval dans la mer*', was my first shared love experience. I was four.

My father's sailing career was no joke. 'I sail to win,' he used to say. Every year, from May to the end of October, he raced *Alphée*, his sleek sailboat named for the Greek river god, most often with the help of his two regular mates, Jean-Claude Guichard and Pierre Girard. There was no question who the captain was, but in case anyone had any doubt, his white captain's cap settled it. They competed on Lake Geneva, but in the summer, many family vacations were organized around international competitions, which required we all travel to Norway, Italy, or Cannes. My father's favorite transporter, Claude Béchard, whom everyone called Léon, would load the boat onto a trailer and tow it to its destination, all over Europe. While my father and his crew raced on the water, my mother and I would play tourists during the day and meet the sailors in the evenings for lively al fresco dinners.

Geneva's climate is tricky, and though there were beautiful summer days, flocks of clouds would often get stuck between the low Jura mountain range and the pre-Alps, creating a dark gray cover that wouldn't lift for weeks. Storms and torrential rains would follow, but they didn't interrupt the sailing races. At the end of such days, my father would appear at the front door in his yellow oilskin suit, balancing the small bags that held his drenched sails.

Always an engineer, he had devised the perfect way to dry the immense spinnakers, the colorful balloon-like headsails he used to distance himself from his competitors. At home, he would tie a corner of the silky spinnaker to one end of the wrought-iron railing on the second floor and run down to tie the other at the bottom, near the front door, transforming the grand stairwell into a triangular grotto of bright red or blue bliss.

I can trace the beginning of my feeble popularity at school to the day he became a world champion. It was the summer of 1972, and the very serious championship for his boat category was taking place on Lake Geneva. There must have been fifteen or more participants, but I knew my champion couldn't lose. I bet against my crush of the moment that my father would win. And he did, leaving none other than the media magnate Ted Turner a mere second.

The bells of the town didn't ring, but they might as well have. Each of the three local newspapers ran the story on the cover page, and one of them even had a banner touting: *Adler à la Barre* – Adler at the tiller. The *New York Times* wrote: 'Ted Turner of the United States has lost his world championship for 5.5-meter yachts to Frédéric Adler of Switzerland'.

I had arrived.

13

Geneva, 1970–1982

MY FATHER WAS FORTY WHEN I WAS BORN. HIS PROFES-
sional success allowed him to relax and realize how busy my mother
was with my three sisters. In a move that was completely out of
character, he asked her how he could help. The six am feeding
seemed like a good idea, since he went to bed early and my mother
read late into the night. For the first time in his life, my father dug
into the nitty-gritty world of child rearing.

'You raised your little head when I came into the nursery,' he
told me, 'and as soon as you saw me, you smiled and stopped crying.'

As soon as I could walk, he'd sweep me away for our *dimanches
matins*, Sunday morning excursions to 'a place you've never been
before'. The regattas started at one pm (to give sailors plenty of time
for mass), so we would leave bright and early. He never asked my
sisters or my mother to come along. The *dimanches matins* belonged

to us. We visited museums and zoos, mountains and river beds, Roman ruins and botanical marvels. Sunday after Sunday, he planted the seeds of my passion for travel and discovery. Year after year, we grew closer, developing an exclusive bond no one could touch. Only when I turned fifteen and started going out on Saturday nights did I lose interest. It happened slowly. He never uttered a word of reproach.

But not all was blissful and easy. He rarely invited me on his boat, insisting that the narrow hull was uncomfortable (it was) and almost impossible to maneuver with just one (junior) sailor (true, except when he participated in the so-called 'solitary regatta', which he often won). But on one August morning, my ninth birthday perhaps, I came downstairs to find both front doors of the house wide open and, on the marble floor, the hull of an optimist – a dinghy built for children – waiting for me, its mast and sails nicely folded next to the gilded mirror.

Pâ was not what one would describe today as a good pedagogue. He must have been gifted as a child because he was completely unable to comprehend not knowing how to do something. Trained at the school of sink or swim, he sent me out in my new boat for the first time on the day of my first regatta. There were two races that day, and I placed last in the first and second to last in the second. I didn't sink, but I never touched the boat again and we never discussed it.

Sometimes on Sunday mornings on our way to our excursion, we would stop at his office in downtown Geneva, where he would dictate into his black recorder or sit at his glass desk and review the documents typed earlier in the week by the secretaries. I loved listening to his exaggerated enunciation as he dictated, pausing regularly to review his last words and add punctuation before moving further.

'Make sure you never learn to type,' he told me, 'or they'll stick you behind a typewriter your whole life.'

While he worked, I would either draw with colored pencils at the other glass desk or wander throughout the empty floor, checking out the photos and posters pinned to the walls of his employees' offices.

One day, perhaps forgetting me for one brief instant, he left his briefcase open on the filing cabinet. Seconds before he slammed the briefcase shut, I registered the cover of a paperback featuring two masculine silhouettes holding hands. I never asked, but I didn't forget.

I never questioned whether my parents were happy together. Not when once, and only once, I heard them fight and my mother insult him. Not when it became clear they rarely spent any leisurely time together, and not when he took me and a group of friends sailing around the Caribbean while my mother took my sisters to the Riviera. Not even when he shared the front cabin with Alain, the blond sailor.

But a few years later, when I saw a stunning young man emerge from my father's car in front of a movie theater where I was meeting a friend, I knew. At first, I didn't move. I gave him enough time to get back to his office, and then I called him.

'I called a while ago and you weren't there,' I said.

'Oh, I just went across the street to pick up something,' he responded.

But he was lying. The movie theater was in a different part of town. A crevasse opened under my feet. I don't remember the rest of our conversation, but I know my friend drove me home. She understood what had unfolded because she, and everyone else, already knew. My mother was playing the piano in the library. I knocked and opened the door. She stopped and took one look at me.

'You know,' she said.

We spoke for a long time. I cried, and she did too. I became an adult that night. When my father came home for dinner, oblivious, my mother took him aside. I have no other memory of the evening, but I decided to leave the next day to visit my cousin Catherine in Paris. Pâ volunteered to drive the seven hours there. In the car, he came out to me. He told me the truth about who he was, his struggles, his double life and my parents' dysfunctional marriage. I stayed away three weeks. Two days after I returned, Upsy, the sweet collie I had received as a gift for my tenth birthday, disappeared. And when Joachim found her, hidden in the middle of the field in the high grasses, she'd been dead a while.

My father spent his entire life attempting to fit into the mold of the domesticated bird his parents and the bourgeois society of the time expected him to be. But the partridge can't survive at the farm. He needs his wings and the sky. Sadly, a prisoner of conventions and society, Pâ would never muster the courage to stand for who he was.

14

Paris, 1925

PARIS, WHERE MY MOTHER ANNE WAS BORN DURING THE Roaring Twenties and where we spent many vacations, felt like a second home. We stayed in a small apartment my mother owned, only a few streets away from the staid Haussmannian building on Villa George-Sand where she grew up.

As a child, from the family home on the second floor of the apartment building, she lifted the heavy curtains to watch her friends play hopscotch in the quiet cobblestoned alley before they yelled for her to join them.

'Who knew higher floors were considered more chic?' she would say to me later.

Anne, or Annette or Annou to her family, grew up within what she insisted was a modest household, between a blond-haired, blue-eyed bon vivant named Daniel who worked as a civil engineer and dreamed of travel and poetry, and Iris, a petite and elegant homemaker, known for her exquisite interpretations of Schubert lieders. Both hailed from La Chaux-de-Fonds, just five miles from the French border, near Neuchâtel in Switzerland, a small town that had become the cradle of the Swiss watchmaking industry. Even though Daniel's grandfather had been a rabbi in nearby Alsace, the couple was completely agnostic. In fact, they didn't even feel Jewish.

Their ancestors, traveling salesmen from Alsace, roamed between France, Switzerland, and Germany until 1833, when the local Swiss authorities officially allowed the Jews to settle in La Chaux-de-Fonds. They had grasped how useful a Jewish international network could be to the budding watchmaking industry. By 1896, the community felt rooted enough to build a stunning Roman-Byzantine synagogue, one of the largest in Switzerland. Later on, Jewish families came to play a crucial role in the development of the town, eventually running some of the more famous brands of watches. Iris and Daniel didn't really know each other as children, even though both families worked for major watchmakers – Iris's for Juvenia and Daniel's for Longines. But Daniel wasn't interested in watches. Fascinated by hydraulic energy, he chose to study engineering in Zürich and later moved to Paris for his career. In 1920, he traveled to Morocco to work on the plans for the first dam in the country. Already a budding poet, he wrote some of his most beautiful prose there.

> *And so it was, as I followed His Excellency El Mokri, between two rows of gleaming bayonets, amongst the roar of artillery bursts mixed with high-pitched fanfare, bugle calls, tambourines and the ululation of the women, in an orgy of noise, color and sun, that I stepped onto the African continent.*

In 1916, Iris Bloch, aged eighteen, was married to Arsène Ullman, a French Jewish man who had immigrated to Brazil and become a wealthy fabric trader. Bravely, she sailed to São Paulo with her mother. The marriage did not last, and just three years later she sailed back with an eighteen-month-old boy named Frédéric.

'What happened?' I asked my mother.

'All she ever said about it was "This was not a man who should have gotten married."'

Iris settled in Paris with her son in 1919, but she had to wait until 1923 to get an official divorce. 'People looked down on her, especially her next mother-in-law,' said my mother.

But when Daniel met her in Paris, he didn't care that Iris was divorced. He loved her voice, her musicality, her cooking, and her son. They married in 1923, near Paris. When my mother was born, at home, at three am, Daniel went to tell Frédéric that a little sister had arrived. Just awakened, he asked, 'Is it a boy or a girl?'

Frédéric was the hero of my mother's childhood. Seven years older than her, he welcomed *la petite soeur* with glee. He invented names for her – she became Trazon or Plonzif depending on the day. They had their own jokes, their own language and their own world, populated with a whole slew of imaginary characters. There was Atanas Brontazou and his cousin Anastase Bircobazou, who traveled the world together but forgot to pack their passports, resulting in adventures with no end. When she misbehaved, he threatened to stop his nightly storytelling visits. Frédéric held her hand as they walked to school. He excelled at the all-boys Lycée Janson-de-Sailly, while Anne was a good student, 'except in math', at the all-girls Lycée Molière. They would part ways on Rue du Ranelagh in the morning, and meet up at the end of the day. Later, Frédéric also excelled at the Ecole Polytechnique, the equivalent of the French MIT.

'My marvelous big brother,' said my mother.

Meals were taken as a family, always accompanied by animated chatter filled with literary and philosophical debate. Iris oversaw the cook, who would prepare homey provincial dishes such as skate roasted in brown butter and capers, or rabbit stew in mustard sauce. But as time went by, the conversations took a more worrisome tone. By 1936, the French population was anxious. The radio resonated with Hitler's speeches.

'I didn't understand what he was saying but he seemed to relish the "ach" sounds as if he was getting ready to spit on the world,' she said.

Anne listened to the adults as they debated the deteriorating European situation. One memory of that time stands out: in May 1937, a massive World Fair, entitled *Exposition Internationale des Arts et des Techniques dans la Vie Moderne*, opened at the Jardin du Trocadéro.

'We went as a family, the four of us,' said my mother. 'For the very first time, I was allowed to go out at night. It was magical to see the new lights in the trees, along the avenues.'

Dozens of countries participated in this international event, but the political tensions were mirrored on the fairground. The German and Russian pavilions stood across from each other menacingly, with the Eiffel Tower as the backdrop. Hitler had only agreed to participate after he managed to get hold of the Russian pavilion blueprints and was convinced his would be taller. The German pavilion was an impressive monster of steel and stone, 177 feet high, topped with the sculpture of an eagle holding a swastika in its claws. The Russian pavilion, covered in marble, was 524 feet long and featured a towering sculpture of a couple holding a hammer and a sickle in their raised hands.

But Anne, who was twelve, remembers best the Dutch East Indies pavilion, where she savored 'My first *café liégeois*,' a sort of coffee milkshake with whipped cream.

She was growing up amongst two contradictory currents. On one hand, her wide-eyed thrill for discovery (literature, nature, tastes, and people), and on the other, the approaching political storm that would engulf the family.

With the annexation of Austria in 1938 and the invasion of Czechoslovakia in March 1939, Nazi Germany continued its dark journey towards European hegemony. But somehow, Daniel and Iris still planned to spend the 1939 August vacation at La Baule, a resort town on the Atlantic Ocean in Brittany. They were still there on 2 September 1939 when, following Hitler's invasion of Poland, France and England had no choice but to declare war on Germany.

15

La Baule, September 1939

WHEN ANNE WOKE EARLY ON 3 SEPTEMBER 1939, THE weather had turned. The family was still at La Stryga, their simple one-story cement vacation rental surrounded by fluffy acacia trees. A few streets away lay the sandy, five-mile-long crescent beach some claimed was the most beautiful in Europe, but the warm sun of August was gone, replaced by gray sky and a wind that seemed to augur winter. She tiptoed to Frédéric's room but he was up already. On the simple bed, a small suitcase lay open.

'Where are you going?' she asked, her heart sinking.

The slight young man known at school for his quick wit and hilarious puns remained silent. He had traded his casual summer shirts for a dark suit and tie, and looked straight at her through his round glasses, but he didn't answer.

The day before, France had decreed *Mobilisation Générale*,

SYLVIE BIGAR

the country-wide call to arms. Large posters were slapped on the
walls of the town announcing that every man belonging to the air,
ground, and sea units was to report to his regiment. People of all
ages gathered in front of the posters. Some argued loudly, some were
quiet. War had come.

For Anne, it meant that her brother was leaving – and no one
but the soldiers themselves knew exactly where they were going. Her
parents remembered the horror of World War I, only twenty-five
years earlier, and feared the worst. In the kitchen, Iris couldn't stop
sobbing, so it was Daniel who took Frédéric to the train station. Anne
stayed behind to try and console her mother. At the exact same time,
all throughout France, men and boys were saying their goodbyes, but
their mood was combative. The soldiers felt strong and the entire
country rallied, eager to show Hitler the grandeur of the French
Republic and its army.

Later, Daniel and Iris spent hours in the family room discussing
the situation. Should they go home or stay in La Baule? With all
the young men gone, Daniel would be needed at his engineering job
in Paris, about 300 miles away, but the relentless bombings of the
capital during World War I loomed in everyone's minds. Finally, it
was decided that Iris and Anne would stay behind. Over the next few
weeks, northern cities and towns along the French–German border
were evacuated, and thousands of refugees poured into La Baule,
including relatives. Seeking some semblance of normalcy, Anne
joined a group of teenage girl scouts, *les éclaireuses*. Soon they were
deployed at the train station with soup and bread for the families
arriving from the east.

'Beside the French nationals, many seemed to come from
Belgium or the Netherlands,' she would later say. 'I felt shy, unable
to communicate with them, so I just smiled and offered what I had.'

Anne was stunned. Her childhood was over.

Along the border to the north, French and German battalions took their positions and watched each other for months, a period later referred to as *La drôle de guerre*, the phony war. Anne missed her brother and her father, she missed her lycée and her friends.

The family unit, now numbering six, moved into Ker Lou Nise, a larger house in La Baule-les-Pins on the outskirts of town. There were several bedrooms on the second floor but Anne often had to sleep in the living room downstairs because one relative or another was passing through and needed shelter.

'I was terrified by the massive oak clock in the living room,' she said. 'It sounded every fifteen minutes, making a croaky, creepy ring.' In October, after Anne turned fourteen, administrators and teachers from Strasbourg in Alsace, near Germany, rallied in a hotel on the Pouliguen harbor to organize classes for the refugees' children. Anne enrolled at what became known as the 'Lycée de Strasbourg evacuated in La Baule'. Classes were held in the bedrooms on three floors. The atmosphere was tense; anxiety fueled the time. Anne hated it.

At the crossroads of childhood and youth, she watched popular sisters Marie-Laure and Yannick Bellon hop on the back of boys' bicycles at the end of the school days and ride away.

'These girls were at ease, they were thin,' she said. 'I swore to myself one day I would be too.' But, hiding in the bathroom, she started eating Côte d'Or chocolate to soothe herself. It had the opposite effect.

The school year passed slowly. Daniel joined the family when his job allowed it and Frédéric spent his military leave in La Baule. By all accounts, the fall and winter period of 1939–40 was one of the coldest in history, one of the reasons why Hitler waited to launch his troops. Finally, on 10 May, Hitler attacked the Netherlands, Belgium and Luxembourg. He crushed the French defenses in a matter of days. The entire country was in shock. The French had trusted their leaders, their army and their superiority, but the assailants couldn't be stopped. The French army retreated and fled alongside a terrified population – young and old – by train, car, bicycle, or foot. Nearly ten million people found themselves on the roads of France while German fighter planes dropped bombs onto soldiers and civilians alike.

Daniel was able to get on a train bound for La Baule. From the classrooms of the hotel/lycée, Anne and her classmates watched a new procession of refugees invade the city, some riding old trucks, carts and bicycles, others walking, carrying suitcases, pushing strollers.

By mid-June, Paris was declared an open city to protect it from being destroyed. France was beaten, it was occupied, and it was stunned.

'The unthinkable happened,' said Anne. 'We thought we were safe, we thought France was strong.'

Surprisingly, Daniel felt that now that the Germans were in Paris, the danger had passed. Thrilled to go home, Anne, Iris, and the rest of the family headed back on 2 July 1940.

'First there was the physical shock of seeing the Nazi flag stretched on the Arc de Triomphe,' said my mother. 'German soldiers with their shiny caps mulling around, the sound of their boots pounding my life.'

Daniel and Iris knew of the raids against the Jews in Germany, Poland, and elsewhere, but they didn't feel concerned, since they were Swiss citizens and weren't practicing. 'Our Christmas tree had always been treated as a grand affair! The gifts, Santa Claus, the *réveillon*.' This term, commonly used in France for both Christmas and New Year's Eve dinners, describes exactly the French gastronomic and social meal UNESCO recently inscribed on the list of Intangible Cultural Heritage. The Kaufmans were leading a thoroughly French life. High Holidays were never mentioned.

'I always envied my friends on their First Communion day, their lacy veils and white organdy dresses,' Anne said. In September 1940, she went back to her beloved Lycée Molière.

'With no television, texting, or web to surf,' she said, 'school, with its social and cultural worlds, was the center of our life.' Anne and her friends plunged into literature and history, reading, discussing, and debating for hours.

'My best friend Anne-Marie Galland, we called her Nanou, and I walked for hours back and forth between our two apartments, unable to interrupt our conversations,' she said. 'From Villa George-Sand to the Passy train station and back.'

The lycée became her mental and emotional escape while the German occupation took stock.

'At the sound of the boots or the *Boches* songs, our wonderful chemistry teacher, Mademoiselle de Leiris, would slam the windows of the classroom shut as noisily as she could.'

One explanation for the derogatory term, which appeared in France around 1860, is a contraction of the word Alboche – al for Allemand and boche from caboche, a head, meant in the sense of headstrong, obstinate.

'I know I shouldn't call them that, but I still can't help it,' she said.

Then came the obligation to register as Jewish at the local police precinct.

'An incredulous red stamp marked Jew in my passport.'

Food became scarce and rumors of roundups more frequent. Frédéric found a job in Toulon, a town on the Mediterranean within the southern free zone, but before he left Paris, he told his parents he intended to join the French Resistance and perhaps de Gaulle in London. Since June 1940, the general, who had fought in World War I, had set up the Resistance headquarters there and spoke daily on the radio to the French population.

'Every evening,' said my mother, 'we would turn on the radio, quietly, to hear de Gaulle and the bells of Big Ben, the melody of freedom and hope. Every evening, the program started with "*Ici Londres, les français parlent aux français*."' (From London, the French speak to the French.)

In June 1942, Anne received the school's Excellence Prize, a reward for the best students. There was a school-wide party and a formal distribution of prizes.

'Even though we were living in this difficult historical climate, I was proud,' she said.

By then Parisians knew that the soldiers 'took' Jews, but Anne, no doubt thanks to her parents' firm belief in their magical Swiss citizenship, felt that she wasn't really at risk, even though an increasing number of friends would suddenly show up at school, devastated when a father or uncle had been 'taken'.

'We didn't use the word "deportation". We didn't know what it meant. We said "taken". We knew prisoners were being sent to camps, but we had no idea what that meant, what happened there.'

And then one night:

'I don't remember hearing the doorbell,' said Anne. 'All I remember was the terrible sound they made. They banged on the door. They yelled for us to open.'

It was 16 July 1942. A few hours before the banging on the Kaufmans' front door, the Gestapo, assisted by the French police, had launched one of the deadliest raids against the Jewish population throughout Paris and the surrounding areas, one in which they took men, women, and children. It became known as the *Rafle du Vel d'Hiv*, for the Vélodrome d'Hiver, a bicycling arena where approximately 7000 of the 12,884 victims, including 4051 children, would be held for three days in the sweltering July heat with barely any food or water and one single toilet, before they were sent to die in the concentration camps.

Days earlier, rumor of an impending roundup had circulated in the Jewish circles. Daniel knew something was brewing. He posted on the front door a letter from the Swiss authorities stating the family was under their protection. The rumor mentioned that women and children would be targeted, so he invited his sister-in-law and Iris's best friend Colette to seek shelter at their home.

'We huddled in the hallway in our pajamas,' said Anne. 'My father said, "Go, take the back stairs, quick." We ran up towards the top floor and the *chambres de bonnes*' – the maids' rooms that often crowned the Belle-Epoque buildings of Paris.

'I cried, "No, they'll take Papa," but he pushed us towards the back exit.'

Daniel sent the women on their way and finally opened the door to what he thought were German soldiers. The men were French. He was stunned when he saw his wife and daughter's names on the grim list the policemen brandished. Since the beginning of the war, he'd held fast to the notion that a wall of safety surrounded their Parisian existence. That night, this nonbeliever, who had never thought to explain to his daughter what Yom Kippur was, realized how wrong he had been. If you were born Jewish, others saw you as a Jew. Swiss or French didn't matter, as long as you were a Jew.

Bravely, he told the policemen that the women had left earlier in the night to line up for bread, as many women were doing. They interrogated him, searched the apartment but never opened the back door. And, miraculously, they didn't take him.

'We'll be back,' they said.

For my mother, life from that point on would forever be sliced in two: before and after that night.

'We spent the next day at a neighbor's apartment on the third floor and then moved to a cousin's home. We didn't know where to go.'

It took eight days of wandering through Paris, from one relative's apartment to the next, until Daniel found a way out for his wife and daughter. The women would require the help of a *passeur*, someone who would smuggle them through the line of demarcation (at that point, the Germans only occupied about half of the French territory). Even then, he still felt that he was not at risk, and that he needed to stay in Paris and keep working.

Anne and her mother took the subway as if going on an errand, and, through a complicated itinerary designed to fool anyone who might be following them, found themselves at the Gare d'Austerlitz and soon on a train headed for Pau and then Mimbaste, a small village in the southwest of France.

'The fear was there, inside, the whole time, but also the pain of leaving my father, Paris, and its pink sky.'

In Mimbaste that very night, they met up with a small group of people, and with the woman who would lead them into a landscape of dunes and high grasses.

'We walked for hours. Suddenly she signaled. We ran, ran behind her. I heard dogs barking in the night. I was terrified.'

All of a sudden, the noise faded: they had crossed the line. At a crossroad, the group was met by three cars that would take them to yet another train station. From there, they rode to Pau in the Pyrenees range. They made their way to Toulon, where Frédéric was working, and stayed with him for two months.

'I hated the palm trees, the fish soup, the ratatouille. I didn't know how lucky I was to be there, what I had been spared.'

By October, it became clear that the Germans would soon be invading the rest of France. Armed with their Swiss passports, the two women prepared to leave for Switzerland.

16

Toulon, October 1942

SLUMPED AT THE WINDOW SEAT IN A TIGHT COMPARTMENT, Anne cried all the way from Toulon to the Swiss border, ten hours away. In her mind, she could still see the slight silhouette of her brother, his hand up, as they pulled away from the station. For weeks now, he had pushed them to leave France, certain that the German forces were about to invade the south.

'Off to Nyffenegger, the Trazon,' Frédéric had joked, a twinkle in his eyes, referring to the famous pastry shop in Lausanne – his attempt to lighten the moment.

'I had this awful feeling, a premonition,' said Anne.

As the sun set on Provence, Anne watched the tall cypresses waver in the evening air as if saluting her pain. The train headed north, stopping several times throughout the night on the way to Vallorbe, the French–Swiss border. Seated next to her, Iris seemed calm and kept her composure. With their Swiss passports in hand, the women were not afraid, just terribly sad.

Fall in the south of France felt just like summer and the compartment was stuffy. Thrown together in this enclosed space, the travelers didn't speak. They couldn't resist the hypnotic rhythm of the train and bobbed along, trying not to touch each other. Someone kept coughing. At each stop, light came back into the wagon, but they kept their heads down. None of them knew the others' circumstances, but they all sensed that this night marked the end of one chapter and the beginning of another.

At the train station in Lausanne, Iris fell into her brother Marcel's arms, finally letting herself go. She sobbed loudly. Embarrassed, Anne felt that the entire station was looking at them. Couldn't her mother make less noise?

'I stopped short in front of a grocery store,' said Anne. 'Bananas. I hadn't seen any in years. I asked my mother if she thought they were real.'

Mother and daughter rented a small room at the Astoria Hotel. Soon, Anne enrolled at Ecole Lémania, the only school in Lausanne that followed the French program, and picked up the preparations for the arduous Baccalauréat, the end of high school exam. At night, she stared at the lights of Evian, the French town famous for its springs, on the other side of Lake Geneva.

'I ached for my beloved France,' she said.

By November, the German army invaded the rest of France and Frédéric moved to Grenoble at the bottom of the jagged and menacing Vercors mountain range, a Resistance stronghold.

In January 1943, the Swiss Legation in Paris sent a letter to Daniel warning that if he (and his mother, who was in a wheelchair) didn't leave quickly for Switzerland, the Swiss authorities could no longer 'guarantee' their safety. In haste, the Bern government organized two different convoys for the 191 Swiss Jews living in Paris. On 1 February, Daniel and his mother boarded the last train bound to neutral Switzerland.

The Kaufman family settled uneasily in Lausanne. In June, Anne passed her Baccalauréat with honors and by October 1943, she had started literary studies at the university. Daniel found a consulting job and Iris, tense with constant worry for her son, made some friends within the Jewish congregation. There was hardly any news from Frédéric, but the family knew he had joined the Resistance full-time.

17

Lausanne, 1944

ANNE WAS PRETTY. A CASCADE OF CHESTNUT CURLS, CLEAR blue eyes, and a plump bosom ensured a slew of admirers. In the two years she spent in Lausanne, first at school and then at the university, she made many friends, and several young men courted her. She was a serious student, passionate about literature and theater, and even though anxiety about the war and her brother's whereabouts was constant, her parents encouraged her to lead a normal life, to enjoy her youth. Throughout the year, she often went out to the movies, or to swing dance.

Anne and her parents returned home to Paris only a few months after the end of the war, one year after the arrival of the thin letter announcing that Lieutenant Frédéric Ullman had been shot and killed in July 1944 with his entire battalion in the Vercors range, near Grenoble.

Anne had finished her master's degree by then and was debating whether to enroll in the 'aggregation', the exam that would allow her to teach at the graduate level.

'I was studying at the Sorbonne library,' she said. 'And suddenly the librarian came to tell me there was a call for me.'

It was her mother, Iris, telling her that Frédéric Adler from Geneva had called and was about to pay them a visit. Anne didn't remember meeting Frédéric Adler at a literary lecture in 1944, but he did – and he was smitten.

The courtship was short. He was handsome, wealthy, and tenacious. He had driven from Geneva in his gleaming 1949 MG. Somehow, he'd been able to snag tickets to a sold-out play she had been dying to see.

'My parents encouraged me to see him, they were thrilled. I thought, if I marry him, they won't have to worry about me anymore.'

They married in October 1949. The wedding pictures show a stunning couple. My father resembles a young, smiling Rudolph Valentino and my mother looks like a brunette Grace Kelly. She smiles too, but there is sadness in her expression. Was it because her brother was absent? Was it because if he had lived, she would not have chosen to marry Frédéric Adler? At the forefront of her mind was the belief that she was helping her parents by marrying this wealthy man.

'It wasn't at all the kind of intimate wedding I would have wanted,' she said. 'We decided to get married in Lausanne, so my maternal grandmother could be there. In the end, she couldn't make it.'

My paternal grandparents led a very social life and they knew hundreds of people. They decided the Beau-Rivage Hotel, one of the most glamorous hotels in the country, would be perfect.

'I would have liked a simpler place, a place with soul, but I didn't say anything, I was intimidated.'

There were hundreds of relatives Anne had never met.

'I was told we had to be careful not to offend anyone, so it was best to invite the entire family.'

The wedding service was celebrated by a rabbi the young couple didn't know. It was in Hebrew from start to finish. Anne didn't understand a thing.

'I didn't like this day. At the end, I felt that my smile was hurting.'

There was no warmth.

'I was immediately unhappy,' said Anne, as she reminisced about the beginning of her marriage. There was disappointment even during their honeymoon in Majorca. Was she a virgin? Was he gentle? A child would make things better, she thought, soon after they came back to Geneva, but it took more than two years for her to become pregnant.

'I was convinced I was sterile,' she said.

She consulted a gynecologist, who prescribed a mix of radiotherapy, shots, and pills. When Jeanine was born, exactly nine months later, Anne was thrilled, but after only a few months she realized she was pregnant again. Already? she thought, but she welcomed another pregnancy, perhaps especially because her husband was so busy, building his engineering practice. A second baby, so quickly, would fill her life.

On 2 November 1952, my parents ate dinner together in their small city apartment. As they were finishing up, my father apologized to his young wife, telling her he needed to return to the office to finish some pressing work. Anne acquiesced, but she was somewhat suspicious. He seemed to need to work late more and more often.

'Part of me believed him,' she said. 'Part of me wanted to believe him.' She put fourteen-month-old Jeanine to bed and ambled back to the bedroom, her round belly slowing her down. She sat on the bed, wondering where her husband was. Suddenly, the phone rang. Anne realized she'd fallen asleep.

'I am awfully sorry to call so late, is this Madame Adler?' asked the man very politely. 'I happen to belong to the third police precinct and I have a message for you from your husband.'

'Excuse me?' asked Anne, a cramp sneaking up through her body.

'Your husband wants you to know that he loves you,' said the police officer. 'That he's sorry, and that he cannot come home.'

'Why, what happened?'

'He's been brought to the can, here in the old town.'

Feeling as if she was about to choke, Anne hung up as soon as she could. She paced back and forth, imagining the worst; she didn't know who to call. Finally she cried herself to sleep and woke up only a few hours later. As soon as the nanny arrived, she got herself dressed and walked to Frédéric's parents' home, a few blocks away.

'I rang the bell,' she said. 'Paul, the butler, opened the door and stood there with his white gloves, stunned to see me at this early hour.'

'I need to talk to Madame,' said Anne.

Madeleine, her mother-in-law, was still in bed, but Anne was shown inside the bedroom. Crying, my mother related the events of the night. Madeleine got up and walked to the chic 'boudoir', her private den decorated by the famous Maison Jensen, to get dressed.

'I knew it,' said my grandmother. 'And you, look at you, pregnant!'

She went to her husband's bedroom. Soon, they were on the phone with their trusted attorney.

Frédéric, then aged thirty, had been arrested in flagrante delicto with another man.

That night, Anne finally opened up to her mother-in-law: when Frédéric asked her to marry him, he told her he had homosexual tendencies. She had taken some time to reflect before giving him an answer, but she didn't tell anyone. Three weeks later, she agreed to become his wife.

'I'll change him,' she thought.

It would take two full days until Frédéric came home, sheepish but defiant at the same time.

'It was nothing, it was nothing, I promise,' he said over and over.

The local papers ran items in the 'arrests' columns. His name only appeared as Frédéric A, but somehow the whole town was abuzz. Anne was devastated. At lunch at his parents' home the next day, she realized she hadn't eaten in days.

My sister France was born three months later.

Even as a toddler, France had a sweet disposition and a kind heart. Later on, at about eight years old, when her eyes started rolling back into their sockets, my parents took her to the family pediatrician.

'Hormones,' he said. 'It will pass.'

It didn't.

She would drop things all the time. And then, while my parents were away one day, she had her first grand mal seizure at age thirteen. It was epilepsy.

'Did something happen when you were pregnant? Did you drop her when she was an infant?' asked the doctor. 'Was there a trauma?'

18

Cap d'Antibes, 1950s

EVERY FEBRUARY, STARTING IN 1949, MY PATERNAL grandparents would leave their home within Geneva's gray brume and drive their Bugatti south towards a vivid Cap d'Antibes, where they rented the Château de la Garoupe, a large Italianate-style villa, until the middle of May. After my sisters were born, my mother would travel south with them and join her parents-in-law for weeks at a time.

One of my favorite photos from that era was taken during lunch, on the veranda. My paternal grandmother Madeleine is presiding under a large straw hat with a red ribbon. She sits, posture perfect in her navy blazer and crisp button-down white shirt, while Paul, the loyal butler in white jacket and gloves, sets the warmed plates on the table. She hasn't lit her first Boyard cigarillo of the day, since that one comes just before dessert. There's a bottle of white wine on one end of the table and a bottle of champagne on the other. My mother Anne, also for some reason wearing a navy blazer and white shirt, seems engrossed in conversation, while my father, young and dashing, is laughing. The terrace lies just off the French doors, but what jumps out at me from that faded photo are the immense wooden shutters, the wicker chairs, the wisteria so lush it seems to crawl inside the house – all silent witnesses to what my three sisters always referred to as the era of la Garoupe. It could have been a movie set.

Built in 1907 for Lady Aberconway, the château and its 55-acre garden popped up on the social map in 1922 when composer Cole Porter discovered the area while serving in the US army and decided to rent it for the summer – a season considered unfashionably hot by the fashionably pale French and British set who wintered there. He didn't come alone. Porter brought along a joyous group of eccentric American bobos that included Scott and Zelda Fitzgerald. In July 1923, their friends Gerald and Sara Murphy joined the crew, convincing the owner of nearby Hôtel du Cap to stay open throughout the summer for the first time. It was this property that would become Fitzgerald's inspiration for the 'rose-colored hotel' set in the first sentence of *Tender Is the Night*.

Porter never returned, but the group would soon welcome Picasso, Fernand Léger, Dos Passos, Hemingway, Man Ray, and Isadora Duncan to name just a few of the many artists and writers who met at Garoupe Beach for picnics and parties. La Côte d'Azur was born. Later on, Picasso would paint one of his most striking works, *Baigneurs à la Garoupe*, set on the beach nearby.

By the time my grandparents arrived, the property had passed on to Lady Norman, Lady Aberconway's daughter, and it occupied half of the eastern part of the Cap d'Antibes. Around the château breathed a magical garden sliced in two by 130 white marble steps that led to the rocks where my sister Jeanine would climb like a fearless goat. This oasis was the epitome of a Mediterranean landscaped garden. Climbing roses made their way along the silvery olive trees; mimosas exploded like particles of sun; forests of purple and white irises grew along the stony paths; dark green cypresses lent their elegant plume, setting off the deep blue of the sea. And the scent! I still remember the scent, a mix of rosemary, lavender, and pine gorging on light.

At la Garoupe, time passed quickly. The days started in my grandmother's bedroom where she met with Susanne, the cook, who came carrying her slate clipboard to evoke various menu possibilities. If the inspiration called for fish, they would often drive to Chez Thérèse, the best fishmonger in the old town of Antibes, to pick up *loups de mer* or *daurades*. In the mornings, a young coach led gym sessions on the lawn, mostly for the women and children since by that time, the men had gone sailing. My grandfather Pierre kept his six-meter in Cannes (his boat measured 33 to 40 feet long; six meters referred to its classification).

At every vacation, my mother, a theater fiend, would create and direct plays, picking actors of all ages from the wide familial pool including my cousins Anne-Marie, Melinda, Stéphane, and Philippe, as well as family friends. One year, it was *The Little Prince*, another *The Jungle Book*. In the evenings, my grandparents entertained often. They played bridge or scrabble, or went out to eat, perhaps at their friend Florence Gould's gorgeous house, La Vigie, in Juan-Les-Pins, a sort of mini-castle I remember was filled with impressionist paintings, the view of the Mediterranean just steps away. For many years after my grandparents had passed away, she kept sending us a box of *calissons*, almond and melon candies, for Christmas.

Throughout my childhood, I often perused the photos and old films shot by my grandmother that recounted the tales of a world that had vanished. I did not know the history of the property, but I sensed how magical that garden was, both wild and neatly planted. As the years went by, it slowly dawned on me just how enchanted the life that my parents and grandparents led there was. Had their life been enchanted, or was it just the decor?

Decades later, it took the Matisse exhibit at the Metropolitan Museum in New York to make me reflect on the degree to which la Garoupe stayed with me. Greens and blues, the primal colors of the Mediterranean region, fill my home. Every January, I scour the flower shops searching for strands of mimosas. My perfume? *Un Jardin en Méditerranée* by Hermès. The perfect vacation has to include water, and I even retraced my steps from Geneva to the Riviera for a gourmand road trip magazine story.

Childhood memories don't only stay with you, they mold you and make you who you are. Surreptitiously, they construct the stage sets of your life, whether you are aware of it or not. Scott and Zelda took their partying elsewhere before their demise, and la Garoupe was sold to a Russian oligarch. The French government has rendered all coastline public, and a high wall now surrounds the magical garden. Overwhelmed with nostalgia a few years after the death of my father, I took my family to Garoupe Beach for a few days, choosing to settle in one of the few hotels that stand just a walk away from the Mediterranean Sea. And while my children splashed happily in the warm sea, I gazed beyond the wall, lost in my own pastel recollections. Just before we left the area, I summoned the courage to ring the bell. No one answered. It was the way it should be, and we all went home.

19

Carcassonne, March 2010

IN THOSE YEARS, EVERY TIME FRIENDS OR COLLEAGUES asked me what I was writing about, I hesitated before dropping what started to feel like a word bomb: cassoulet.

'Cassoowhat?' some would respond, staring at me interrogatively.

But it was worse for those who knew what it was, as their stare would carry a blend of pity and disbelief.

'You're writing about cassoulet *again*?'

'So where did you taste one?' I would ask, trying to move the conversation along. Then, invariably, their eyes would get a tad misty and they would offer their own memories of the best cassoulet they ever had.

'It was a *relais routier* (the equivalent of a truck stop) near Bordeaux, I just thought I'd give it a try, oh my!'

'A friend insisted we go to this old cafe in Paris and it was the *plat du jour*, she said it was a must.'

'I had my first cassoulet in Baton Rouge, who knew.'

And then they'd wink and make a funny face. Because everyone knows beans make you fart.

Even author Prosper Montagné relayed his surprise as he arrived at a shoe cobbler in Carcassonne one winter morning to find it shuttered. Fearing a death in the family, he walked up to the door only to find a sign saying, 'Closed due to cassoulet'. Was the cobbler cooking one, or had he savored it the night before and was still coping with the aftermath?

'Not every bean makes you fart!' cried Garcia, back in the kitchen at Domaine Balthazar towards the end of my *stage*. 'And not if it's cooked properly!'

It was difficult to hear him clearly. The reservation book for that evening called for a full house. Garcia and Guy were on fire, and the noise was deafening. On the stove, vats of broth filled with bones, chunks of vegetable, and fresh herbs bundled together billowed into clouds of hearty steam I wanted to roll in. We were making veal stock for the meat sauces and earthy pork stock redolent of forests and meadows for the cassoulet. Time and heat transformed the light broth into a more intense stock, some of which we spooned out, to shepherd it gently – more time, more heat – towards the syrupy nectar called demi-glace that adds depth and presence to any dish.

Fish bones and langoustine carcasses flew between gurgling water and flame. Some would end up as fish stock; others, the lucky ones, would get anointed into bisque, the most intense, creamy fish potage and one of the best soups of the French repertoire. But I was not making bisque and I was not making sauce. I peeled carrots, potatoes, and more onions. I washed and chopped celery. That week, I learned to cut dead animals and watched the chefs roast their remains. How could death smell so good?

I kept my nose in the task of the moment and tried to make myself useful, but I was overwhelmed. Until then, I hadn't paid much attention to the rest of the menu. The restaurant offered a whole array of classic dishes. There was monkfish from Brittany, tender lamb confit with thyme flowers, seared foie gras, almost liquid, and foie gras terrine, luscious and salty, veal sweetbreads sprinkled with muscat wine. I had never really gauged how much work went into preparing for show time.

Beans were everywhere: bags of dry ones, others floating in pots, *cassoles* of all sizes lining the counters and filled to the brim with soupy beans and scorching stock into which we pushed pieces of duck confit, roast pork, and sausage.

'Not like that,' Garcia would mutter. '*Regarde*,' he'd say.

And that's what I did. Oh, I learned plenty of tricks. I learned to use a knife properly, learned to watch for burns and scrub the counters, but, most importantly, I watched Garcia.

The chef was convinced that most cooks didn't know what to do with beans, which he considered one of the pillars of his regional cuisine. Why did he finally decide to share some of his knowledge with me? Perhaps because I was interested in the whole picture – the history, the theories, the kitchen. One afternoon, we sat down with a bean grower for a culinary history course.

'Think of Prosper Montagné's *Festin Occitan* as our newest Testament,' said Marcel Langdone, who owned acres of bean plants near Castelnaudary. '*Maître* Montagné wants to believe that cassoulet emerged at the beginning of time, but he knows that beans only arrived in Europe after they were discovered in the Americas, and that this proves the dish could not have been invented before.' Langdone explained it was Catherine de Medici, born in Florence and promised in 1531 to the future Henri II, who brought to France in her dowry teams of Italian cooks and containers of beans.

But the fava bean, he continued, landed in Europe from the Middle East with the crusaders in the thirteenth century and, back then, cooks used the fava (or *fèves* in French) for a stew that could be considered the ancestor of cassoulet and was called *fèvoulet* or *fèvoulade*. And it doesn't stop there. Montagné also quotes historians who mention cassoulet emerging with the Arabs in the seventh century and who cooked a stew made with mutton and some kinds of beans. We were going back in time and I was intrigued. What was the place of the beans in Jewish cooking, I wondered.

But before I could ask, the men were arguing about which bean was best for cassoulet. Oh no, I thought, here we go again.

In *Beans, A History*, author Ken Albala writes that 'nearly every place on earth has its own native species and nearly every culture has depended on beans'. Back in my hometown in the 1970s, Madame Comte at the produce shop sold some, but we never bought them. My mother couldn't stand beans and she didn't remember her mother ever cooking any. When I asked her why her mother cooked lentil soup but not beans, her tone turned condescending. 'I think my brother ate them at boarding school and hated them,' she said.

Indeed, Albala mentions 'class-based antagonism'. Beans, one of the best sources of vegetal protein, were for centuries associated with peasant food. But while in Europe wealth often guaranteed access to meat, beans and their legume cousins still held a central place on menus, both at home and in restaurants in India and South America. Albala also mentions the link between etiquette and the flatulence produced by the gut bacteria processing the dried beans. At home, bodily functions were never discussed and I never heard my parents fart. Fresh string beans, however, do not cause any fanfare; a much safer bet at the table of Jewish bourgeois striving to appear elegant.

Cassoulet created serious dissent among its subjects, even in terms of which beans to use. Most cooks favored the Tarbais bean, an ancient specimen from the town of Tarbes, close to the Spanish border, that grows along corn stalks and was revived in the 1980s. The Tarbais is the only bean that achieves the distinction of 'label rouge', a sort of culinary gold medal that guarantees the quality of its taste. Picked by hand, the pods are dried in the sun until the farmer shakes one of them to see if the bean 'sings'. Only then can they be hauled into the machine that separates the pod from the bean, then checked against regulations and standards to ensure that they can be named Tarbais.

The essential quality of the Tarbais bean is a delicate skin that will not burst, even if it is cooked for a long time, but Garcia (of course) had a different opinion.

'Why would I go all the way to Tarbes for a bean?'

Garcia worked with the local lingot, which he considered the easiest to digest but also the one that keeps its shape the best during the cooking process. He argued (of course) that the lingot had been used in cassoulet since the sixteenth century and that was that.

'Why would I use a bean from Tarbes?' he barked. 'Cassoulet wasn't invented there.'

20

Carcassonne, March 2010

'CAPITALE MONDIALE DU CASSOULET', READ THE ROAD SIGN
at the entrance of the town of Castelnaudary, about 15 miles from
Carcassonne. The self-proclaimed 'cassoulet capital of the world'
made no secret of its purpose in the universe. A nondescript *centre-
ville* was home to a hotel named La Maison du Cassoulet, and there
were restaurants with names such as Le Cassoulet Gourmand, Au
Vrai Cassoulet and Restaurant Marty Cassoulet. And there was
more. As we headed towards the western edge of town, we came
upon one of the annoying roundabouts that seem to have sprouted
all over France and do little but slow traffic down, so that one can
actually hear what the truck driver giving you the finger is saying.
This one was different. At its center stood a 16-foot-high cast iron
statue of a woman with no face but carrying a massive terracotta
bowl – perhaps the world's biggest *cassole*. Named *La Porteuse de*

Cassoulet (the cassoulet carrier) and inspired by an ancient postcard, it was crafted by a local artist named Jean-Claude Sabaté and inaugurated in 2007 with great fanfare. This was the official emblem of the world capital of cassoulet.

Garcia had pulled more strings and I had been allowed to visit one of the numerous factories based in Castelnaudary that manufacture some of the staggering 70,000 tons of canned cassoulet produced and devoured each year in France. Does 'cassoulet in a can' conjure images of viscous Chef Boyardee ravioli, or maybe red cans of corned beef? France is another world. In France (as in many other European countries), tin cans can hold delicious foods with followers almost as passionate as cassoulet lovers. Over the past decade in Europe, canned sardines have enjoyed a vast resurgence. The industry was first developed in southern Brittany during the first half of the nineteenth century: sardines were cooked briefly in olive oil, stuffed in clay jars named *oules* and sealed in more oil, a system quite similar to the one used to make duck confit. By 1824, a confectioner named Joseph Colin created the first sardine-canning factory in Nantes using the tinning process developed by a colleague, Francois Appert. Throughout the nineteenth and even the twentieth century the industry grew tremendously, and the sardines were always marketed as a luxury product. In 1879 alone, France produced 82 million tins. Today, the canning factories (often owned by the same family for generations) have modeled their marketing campaigns on the wine industry. They have hired famous illustrators and artists to create romantic labels that suggest authenticity and artisanal practices, and hired PR firms to create the concept of 'vintage sardines'. Collectors are appearing out of nowhere with cans dating back decades. After all, like wine, the fish only gets better as time goes by – if one doesn't forget to turn the cans regularly to moisten the flesh.

In the United States, however, canned food suffers from a bad rep, something that has resulted in one of the worst translations of a French recipe: the original *salade niçoise*. Born in Nice in the South of France, the dish historically included only tomatoes, olives and canned anchovies with olive oil and salt. Canned tuna was added next, and rumor has it that Auguste Escoffier (1846–1935), the first chef to organize professional kitchen teams and advocate for seasonal ingredients, took it upon himself to add boiled potatoes and string beans. When I arrived in New York in the 1980s, I was horrified to see seared fresh tuna instead of the delicious canned tuna packed with olive oil. How can fresh tuna, a product of nouvelle cuisine but more often than not of poor quality, be superior to traditional canned tuna packed in olive oil? It doesn't make any sense, and completely denatures the traditional recipe.

But at the factory in Castelnaudary, it was all about tradition. Or at least, so I was told. I was welcomed by a group of suits who insisted on speaking English with me, and whose long discourse set out to convince me that cassoulet in a can was truly traditional, artisanal, and authentic. These key words of the food industry marketing efforts strive to convey images of ancient buttery bliss, but I wasn't easy prey. I wanted to inhale the herbs and watch the beans swell; I wanted to hear fat sizzling in the pans.

I was told to don a white lab coat, plastic boots, and a cap, and to follow the men inside. The visit took about seven minutes. I saw nothing. I smelled nothing. Nothing but room after room filled with machines roaring, bubbling, and creaking. Empty jars rolled on ribbons of plastic, pretty labels flew under the ceilings and steam billowed from covered vats. I never saw any food.

Garcia took one look at me when I arrived at the kitchen the next day and went back to cutting onions. We never discussed cans again. Later, on Ranker.com, I would stumble on a list of the twenty most disgusting canned foods, and there, alongside 'Manhattan style fish assholes' and 'canned creamed possum', was duck fat – the key ingredient of cassoulet. The chasm between the two worlds I was attempting to bridge was both cultural and gastronomic.

'Fat is flavor. Fat is pleasure,' said the chef.

He made his own duck fat, of course, which meant that he rendered the plump legs of fattened ducks (*les canards gras*) raised for foie gras, and then stored the meat within some of the white goop, collecting the rest in the refrigerator. French home cooks buy glass jars of duck fat, which they use pretty much like butter or vegetable oil.

'Fat is good for you, especially duck fat,' said Garcia. He was referring to the so-called French paradox, a set of medical data gathered in the 1980s that contrasted the amount of animal fats ingested by the inhabitants of southwestern France with their incredibly low rate of heart disease. At the time, wine makers jumped in, declaring that surely it was the wine that saved the hearts of the populations. Cheesemongers claimed that cheese was the savior, but many others were convinced that the true hero was duck fat, because it is monounsaturated and even more unsaturated than chicken or turkey. Today, it appears this correlation may have been a bit far-fetched. Suffice it to say that duck fat is the secret behind the tastiest and crunchiest fries I've ever made.

'Fat is treated as if it is Satan,' Garcia said. 'After a day in the fields, no one got indigestion because of a cassoulet dinner. Our lifestyle has changed.' So now that so many of us lead sedentary lives, should we filter the fat out of the old recipes? I asked timidly.

'Eat a bit less, *ma fille*,' he said. 'Don't take the flavor out of life.'

21

Geneva, 1970s

MY ROOM AT BEAU-CHAMP WAS THE ONLY BEDROOM THAT opened on the street side. It made sense (first come, first served) that my three older sisters would have the view, and even decades after they had left home, their bedrooms continued to be named for their initial occupants. During the summer holidays, my daughter always stayed in France's room.

In fact, I loved my small corner room. We lived on the main street called Rue du Village, and I relished being able to watch the comings and goings in the small village. Across the street, in my early years, stood a barn that housed as many as thirty cows. I climbed and sat on the radiator that ran along my window and listened to the soundtrack of their lives – their moos, their hooves on the hay-covered floor. Whenever I could, I would run there in secret and pet the soft forehead of the giant animals, letting them lick my palms with their coarse tongues.

Perched at my window, I would also observe the Sunday crowds shuffling into the Protestant temple at the end of the street. Its bells set the rhythm of our life, especially the Sunday morning call to mass, but also the carillons on Saturday afternoons that announced a wedding. 'Quick, let's go see the bride.' Even though we lived next to the church and some villagers called our house 'the castle', I felt we didn't belong. We didn't go to church and I never frequented the village school.

At the time, our village held three shops. On our street, just across from the fountain framed by begonias and red geraniums, Madame Comte, short, round with an open face and blondish curly hair, specialized in produce and resembled the apricots she sold. I knew there had been a Monsieur Comte, but he was dead or gone by the time I began accompanying our cook to get fruits and vegetables. Next door stood a bakery where we bought the so-called *pain anglais* – English bread, a sort of sweet white pullman used for my father's toast. My favorite treat was a flaky, golden pear turnover we called *rissole aux poires*, but I was even more interested in the Bazooka chewing gums my sister Jeanine and I enjoyed. We would share the comics folded inside and then she would teach me how to blow bubbles, an art I still practice today.

Only a few steps away, the third store was called La Laiterie (the dairy) and it specialized in milk and cheese. The bakery was the first to close, perhaps because the Laiterie sold bread too, and no one revived Madame Comte's boutique after she died. The Laiterie agonized for many years until it closed for good, a victim of the supermarkets and malls in nearby towns.

I always loved good food. The next treat or the next meal was often on my mind. One night, I woke with a cookie craving long after the grown-ups had gone to bed. My father had held a work reunion in our dining room earlier that day, and I wondered if there were any cookies left. Even though I wasn't hungry, the texture of the buttery shortbreads dotted with hazelnuts haunted my tastebuds. I got up and, in my pajamas, opted for the staff staircase to be sure I wouldn't wake my parents. But the old steps creaked loudly under my feet. Annoyed but determined, I opened the door to the dining room and stopped short. Both windows were wide open, and the white curtains were blowing outside. The doors to the low credenza were ajar and the carpet was covered with our collection of silver bowls and platters.

Odd, I thought. Had there been a need to air them out? What could have had happened? I resolved to wake up my parents. I climbed back upstairs and knocked on their door, first softly and then louder and louder until my father said: '*Entrez!*'

'Pâ,' I asked timidly, 'did you take out the silver to be aired out?'

'What are you talking about?' he said, visibly annoyed.

'Well, someone broke in, then.'

He jumped up, eyebrows and silk pajamas all wrinkled, and followed me downstairs where he was forced to agree. We had been burglarized. Everyone woke up and the police came. Soon I was sent to bed, but not before, while the grown-ups were busy, I stole some of the cookies from the rectangular glass jar.

22

Geneva, 1970s

WHEN DID I KNOW THERE WAS SOMETHING WRONG WITH Michèle, the youngest of my three sisters? We were eight years apart. Before I was born, she had been the baby, the sweet, quiet child my maternal grandfather described as a 'charming little elf'.

I know we went on family vacations; there were many lazy weekends, many meals. But, looking back, I remember so little about her. Once on a trip to Canada, we shared a room. Was I ten or eleven? All I know is that it did not go well. She refused to turn the light off to let me sleep at my normal time, she called her friends and chatted for hours in the bathroom so I wouldn't hear. She watched me undress, looking at me in a strange way, and she seemed furious most of the time. I told my parents I could never do that again, that she scared me. They tried to convince me that the problem was mine, that I needed to accept her and understand her.

In another memory, we are in the house's formal library, surrounded by about five thousand books arranged by subject: poetry, theater, classic literature, contemporary fiction, and World War II history. We are fighting about which television channel to watch. I can see us screaming at each other and then, suddenly, we are down on the ancient parquet and she's scratching my arms while my mother runs in yelling for her to stop.

My three sisters went to elementary and middle school at a nearby Catholic institute. At fourteen, Michèle switched to the public system in downtown Geneva. She was studious, chose Latin and German as her required languages. Our mother would spend hours helping her with homework every night.

At thirteen, I asked my parents if I could host my first dance and they agreed. They had been quite strict with my sisters. I was told that when Jeanine, the oldest, went to Israel for a discovery trip at eighteen, our father told her he would disown her if she lost her virginity before she got married. But they had evolved since then. They had sailed through the 60s, and they agreed with me that teenagers should have disco parties and dance under dimmed lights.

Our cook at the time was Helene, a jolly, round lady from Portugal whom I remember most for her smooth, creamy ham croquettes. The night of my party, busy in the kitchen, she saw Michèle from the corner of her eye, quietly releasing the largest knife from the magnetic holder on the wall before heading back up to her room. Helene immediately called our parents, using the internal phone system.

Down in the basement, things were in full swing. We danced to the Beach Boys and Supertramp. The color bulbs flashed in rhythm, and all I could think of was whether my secret crush, Stefan, would invite me to dance once the slow songs started.

At some point in the evening I decided lipstick would help, so I ran up from the basement into the kitchen and opened the door to the hallway. The flashing lights of the ambulance bathed the whole house in red. Two men wearing white coats were coming down the staircase, holding Michèle in a beige straightjacket. The rest of the night is a blur. Terrified and ashamed, I tried pushing the image down from my brain. All I could think was: please, please, make sure no one sees this!

Was there a family discussion about what happened? Did I know what she attempted? When was I told? Here again, I have no memory of any open talk. In fact, none of my friends had any inkling of what had transpired that night, and I pushed it down so hard that I forgot about it for years.

When Michèle came home from the psychiatric clinic, several months later, and in the ensuing years before I moved out, my parents tried to minimize her mental health problems. Whenever we both spent time at Beau-Champ, she seemed to harbor a deep hatred for me, one stemming from jealousy. We never spoke about it, but I knew that before I was born, she had been the favorite child and that I had stolen that from her. As the doctors tuned her medication up or down, she was more or less aggressive, more or less lethargic, but as the years went by, I kept my distance.

Until one morning many years later, when the phone rang in the chalet I occupied with my boyfriend, Gregori. That day we were due to leave for New York, where I had been accepted at Columbia University. I had asked my mother to drive us to the airport.

'*Allo?* Sylvie?' said my mother. 'Listen, Michèle is offering to drive you.'

'What?' I said. 'No way.'

'Come on, she's been doing so well. She wants to be helpful. It will be good for your relationship.'

'No,' I said. I wasn't sure why, but my instinct told me to refuse. My stomach tightened.

'You're being incredibly selfish. For once, she's reaching out to you. Please, let her.'

I tried to stand up to my mother, but she was formidable, and she convinced me. Soon after, Michèle appeared in our driveway. She was thin then, and wore tight denims tucked into beige tall leather boots. She looked at me hard and my heart sank.

We placed our suitcases in the trunk and, against my best judgment, I got into the passenger seat while Gregori sat in the back. She seemed angry but calm as we snaked our way out of the village.

Then we hit the highway and, all of a sudden, she pushed on the accelerator pedal.

'Finally, I have you,' she said. 'I'm going to crash the car and send you to paradise. Finally, I'll get rid of you.'

'Stop,' I screamed, watching the road and the high wall flashing by, closer and closer. Terror had seized me. I couldn't die like this, at nineteen. Nausea brought liquid up to my mouth as I gripped the doorhandle, but reaching in between the two front seats, Gregori pulled on the emergency brake. The car went spinning – it's the end, I felt – and then stopped, miraculously without hitting the wall or any other car. I pushed the door open and jumped out as Gregori shoved Michèle hard, away from the driver's seat.

Gregori told me later that he and Michèle spoke and that he calmed her down. He said that she quickly became sheepish and apologetic. Back in the car, Gregori took the wheel and convinced me to sit next to him (it took some time; I was shaking all over). In the back, Michèle stayed silent. As soon as we pulled in front of the airport, I got out and ran to the check-in line, then went through customs without waiting for Gregori. At the gate, once he'd joined me, I dialed the house from a pay phone and told my mother what had transpired.

'You're lying,' she said. 'That's impossible, she couldn't have done that.'

That was the ultimate betrayal. How could I have made that up? I put the receiver down and boarded the plane to New York and the rest of my life.

23

Provence, summer 2003

THE YEAR 2003 TURNED OUT TO BE A GREAT YEAR FOR WINE. In July, Europe emerged from a wet spring into one of the most intense heatwaves in decades. There was no air conditioning in the hospital room where my father lay, and as I stared out the window, the gray silhouette of the Salève mountain appeared blurry, as if the air itself was gasping for more oxygen.

Earlier in June, Michael and I had rented La Bastide, a traditional stone house in Provence, just outside the village of Bonnieux. Painted yellow with green shutters and a brick roof, the two-story 'mas' hid at the back of a long private road shaded by century-old oak trees. Zoe was almost two. Seated on the mossy steps that led from the wisteria-covered veranda to the suspended garden, she resembled a malicious cherub lost in a watercolor. She ran around the old basin, played hide and seek with a moody toad and dipped her little toe in the cool water. In the wide courtyard she sat seriously on the gravel and examined each pebble as if it hid a tiny treasure. But I couldn't run with her or sit on the grass. Even though I was only six months pregnant, the baby in my belly hung low and pressed on my spine at regular intervals.

When we first arrived, I felt well enough to organize daily trips to the markets and the surrounding hill towns, but the pain mirrored the crescendo of the heat and by the middle of June, even a short car trip was excruciating. Taking painkillers was out of the question as they could harm the baby, so after a few sleepless nights, we headed to a local chiropractor.

'Is there anything else happening in your life?' asked the gentle balding man in a white lab coat. 'How do you feel about this baby coming?'

'I am thrilled,' I said bravely. 'I am amazed I am carrying a boy, amazed that my female body knows how to create a boy, how to make a penis.'

The chiropractor smiled but pushed on.

'What else is hurting?'

Instantly, tears started rolling down my cheeks. 'My father is dying,' I whispered. He had been sick with leukemia for several years, but this was the first time I had voiced what was happening.

'That's what's hurting,' he said, taking my hand. 'Not the baby. Where is he? Go to him.'

Back at La Bastide that night, I called my parents.

'Oh, Sylvie, he's in the hospital,' said my mother. 'I didn't want to interrupt your vacation.'

He'd been diagnosed in August 1998. I could never pinpoint exactly when that nasty cough started, but it lingered past the winter and way into the spring, then summer. Michael and I had spent some time with my parents at a mountain music festival where we hiked the high meadows during the day and listened to classical music in the evenings. Besides the cough, he had seemed in great shape. The morning we flew back to New York, he was meeting with his doctor, so as soon as I cleared customs, I looked for a pay phone and called him collect.

'Don't worry,' he said. 'I have lymphoma.'

'What's that?' I asked, my stomach cramping.

'A blood issue, but it's not serious.'

He was lying, of course. In those pre-Google days, it took a while to find out the truth. It was leukemia. He just thought the term lymphoma sounded less threatening.

The disease bided its time for a while, but within a few years, my father needed dialysis, at first once a week, then twice. I traveled home as much as I could by myself and then, after Zoe was born in 2001, with a little girl strapped to my chest. Pâ saw this battle like a regatta he needed to win. With me, he always did his best to sound reassuring.

But by July 2003, things had taken a turn for the worse. He had pneumonia. In view of the finish line, the disease was preparing its final assault. We left Provence early and I rushed to the hospital.

His smile when I pushed open the door to his room said it all. His love. His relief. His gratitude, as if I somehow had the power to change things. He was propped up in his bed, thinner and grayer but still so handsome in his dark gray silk pajamas. I sat on his bed and he put his hand on my belly. We both cried.

The next day, he agreed to get out of bed and, leaning on my shoulder, walked a few steps. My mother, my oldest sister, and my cousin were there, bringing him food, newspapers, and books. He was not in pain, but the heat was unbearable. The pain in my back made me hunch, like an old woman. It was so much easier to complain about the lack of air conditioning and my back than to face the actual battle in the room.

Thankfully, after a few days, his normal color returned, and he was able to breathe more freely. Soon he was walking the whole length of the corridor and back. One morning, I found him outside with a nurse, sitting in his Chinese robe, in the shade. The doctors started talking about him going home.

The next thing I remember is him lying in the large bed at home, on his left side, huddled and cold under the heavy blanket.

'What's the hardest thing?' I asked him.

'Having no hope left,' he whispered.

It was the end of July and time for me to return to New York. The baby was due in October. We talked about my coming back towards the end of August, but I wasn't sure I'd be able to, or even want to for fear of giving birth on the plane. The morning I left, he insisted on getting up to say goodbye, and followed me into the hallway. He leaned on the intricate wrought-iron banister as I descended the staircase.

'Bon voyage,' he said, in tears.

You too, I thought.

The month of August passed quickly. Between my work and Zoe, I was busy. I was getting bigger, and walking more slowly.

I did not plan another trip.

By then, my father needed dialysis three times a week and his body was slowly shutting down. In early September, he started having trouble breathing and the doctor diagnosed another bout of pneumonia. He was admitted to the hospital, and phone conversations became difficult. His elocution was blurred but still I called every day, even when I could no longer understand him. Until the day my sister told me he had opted out of the third dialysis of the week.

'You know what that means?' Jeanine asked me.

I didn't answer.

There was one more phone call. He was speaking breathlessly, and I could not understand a word he was saying. Then he fell asleep and all I could hear was snoring.

I listened for a long while and, finally, hung up.

My mother's call woke me on 27 September.

'*C'est fini*,' she said. It's over.

It was impossible to travel back home for the funeral: I was nine months pregnant and no airlines would allow me on board. It was the perfect excuse.

24

New York, July 2010

'PARTRIDGE,' I MUTTERED TO MYSELF. '*POUR L'AMOUR DE Dieu*, where am I going to get partridge?'

Outside, the thermometer read 90 degrees Fahrenheit and the pavement was literally melting, spawning the familiar acrid smell of urban summers, but as I watched the yellow cabs stream beneath the window of my Manhattan apartment, I felt I had no choice. I'd been back a few months already and my friends were clamoring for a cassoulet. A dozen of my foodie friends were due to show up the next weekend, ready for a gargantuan feast. Seated at the zinc counter in my sleek kitchen, I glanced at the handwritten page gifted to me by Eric Garcia and all I could see was 'partridge'. I felt the impossibility of the mission. The bird is an essential ingredient in his, I mean in *the*, cassoulet recipe, and there was no way I was going to find one at my local Gristedes, let alone hunt one between now and next week.

Maybe I could use a different bird? Skip the ingredient altogether? Find a different recipe? Could I betray him? The page, with Garcia's round and regular handwriting and its naive drawings, felt like an ancient treasure map. Seemingly simple, it hid a lifetime of experience. Except for that bird, I felt pretty confident I could replicate his cassoulet, even though I hadn't touched a bean in months.

Suddenly I wondered what Julia Child's take on cassoulet was. After all, she fell in love with French cuisine and found a way to 'translate' it for the American audience. I went to my office upstairs and found my old copy of *Mastering the Art of French Cuisine*. Cassoulet, page 399.

In the numerous pages dedicated to the stew, she explained that even though the dish is rooted in the fabric of the region, there are, as is often the case in France, many opinions as to what constitutes a cassoulet. *Had she met Garcia?*

Okay, that was fine, but she went on to declare in her typical independent Julia Child way, that a delicious cassoulet could be prepared in any location with beans and any of its usual meats. She never mentioned partridge! I breathed a sigh of relief. She called for Polish sausage, Northern white beans, and breadcrumbs for the crust. Oh no! I could almost hear Garcia's ire.

I sat back down and took a deep breath. Come on, I thought. I am in New York and he is most probably in Carcassonne, nose deep in the fragrant stock. Finally, I knew what to do. I would make both recipes for my friends. Then, they would taste and judge.

Problem number one. My kitchen had lots of pots, many of them acquired during a stint as a recipe tester for a celebrated food writer. I opened my largest cabinet and stared at what I had considered my prize pot: a tarnished orange Le Creuset Dutch oven made in cast iron that had belonged to Iris, my maternal grandmother. I didn't own a *cassole*. Dread.

Quickly I went back upstairs to my library and searched the shelves – a very lengthy process, since I owned about 600 cookbooks. I could picture it, the image of a massive *cassole* that graced the cover of a book called *The Cooking of Southwest France* by Paula Wolfert. She was the first American writer to delve into the cuisine of Morocco in the 70s, and then, in 1983, the southwest of France, literally introducing duck confit and cassoulet to American cooks. I didn't know Paula, but a colleague gave me her number.

I found the book, re-read her recipe and then dialed, introducing myself and explaining the dire situation. Paula got it immediately. She didn't think there was anything weird about being obsessed with cassoulet. She told me she lugged a *cassole* home to Napa all the way from the Vat factory and then found an enthusiastic potter in Minnesota who was game to replicate it.

'So, in fact you got a *grésale?*' I asked.

But she didn't seem to hear me as she gave me the potter's number. That night I dreamed of men in red robes burning me at the stake, and pots breaking over my head.

I felt I was cheating on Garcia as I called the potter the next day. And a few days later, not one but two glorious *grésales* landed in my Manhattan kitchen.

In the meantime, there were more problems. Of course, saucisse de Toulouse is nowhere to be found. Nor are ribbons of pig skin. A pig skull? Fuhgeddaboudit! There are, however, a variety of beans available – just not cassoulet-specific haricots lingots. For meats, the local butcher can only offer ridiculously lean pork loin and lamb shank, not pig feet or lamb shoulder.

Time to get creative. I called Ariane Daguin, the daughter of André Daguin, one of France's legendary chefs, credited for inventing the recipe for duck magret at his two-Michelin-star restaurant in Auch, Gascony. Ariane grew up deboning ducks, rendering duck fat, and cooking game birds. After coming to New York and attending Columbia University, she launched D'Artagnan, which, thirty years later, has become the premier purveyor of hard-to-find French ingredients in the United States.

Beans? Ariane could only offer haricot Tarbais, favored by many cassoulet experts but again, anathema to Eric Garcia. I imagined his disapproval but ordered them anyway. For Julia Child's version I chose Great Northern beans.

Day one of the cooking offers few opportunities for error. Retracing in my mind the steps I took in the kitchen in Carcassonne, I cut open the white fabric bag and let the beans drop into the colander I placed in the sink. The cold water flows through them, rinsing away the impurities and the small stones. Running my hands through them feels almost sacred, as if I was caressing prayer beads. I leave them in a bowl of water where they will soak overnight. I roast veal and beef bones as well as carrots, onions, and leeks. I tie herbs and celery branches into a giant bouquet garni. I add the ham hocks I found at a Jamaican butcher in Brooklyn, and everything goes with water into the largest stockpot I own while Garcia's words resonate in my mind: 'Everything in life stems from the stock.' The slow simmer of the broth summons a vision of victory; I imagine parading my new dish and the new 'me' into a room filled with friends and family.

But day two brings signs of trouble. The stock, only yesterday a source of hope, is far too fatty. The beans are too big. Their skins begin to rupture. I distract myself by searing the sausage into the duck fat, which smells odd. I render the pork rind and cook the beans. Finally, I assemble the ingredients in the *cassole*. Beans first. Then meats. After adding some stock, I slide the dish into the oven.

Out of sight does not mean out of mind. I fret about failure. I pour a glass of Madiran. I stare at the oven door and pray for the formation of a crust.

When I pull the cassoulet from the oven a few hours later, there is no crust in sight. The beans have turned to mush. The entire dish is drying up. I add stock and cook it some more, but the dryness persists. I weigh my options. Throw it out and start again? Not enough time. Phone a friend, maybe Daniel Boulud, to make one for me? Impractical. And embarrassing. My only option is to do whatever I can to save my cassoulet. I scramble. One more day and my guests will be ringing the bell.

To save my cassoulet, I put my pride aside and call France as early as I can the next morning. It's my lucky day – Garcia picks up and jumps right in. He asks about my ingredients. Haricot lingot de Pamiers? *Non*. Pig skin? *Non*. Partridge? *Non*. He suggests adding duck fat. I say that I have already tried. 'What time are people coming?' he asks. For lunch in a few hours. How many? Twelve. After a long silence, the Frenchman says, 'Are they French?' *Non*. 'They won't know the difference,' he says, and hangs up.

The chef is right. My friends love both versions. Most ask for seconds. I take one bite and feel sick. The taste is closer to the canned cassoulet from Castelnaudary than the authentic version from Carcassonne. Seated at a celebration of the success of my quest, I feel like an impostor.

25

New York, 2011

AS FAR AS MY FRIENDS AND FAMILY WERE CONCERNED, I WAS
done with this funny obsession with cassoulet.

'Wouldn't it be great if you wrote about, hmm, deeper things?'
asked my mother.

But to her chagrin, I wrote about a fish shop in the Hamptons
where Martha Stewart rubbed shoulders with Warren Buffett
and Richard Gere, a Manhattan churro joint created by a Spanish
attorney who couldn't live without churros, and a tiny village in the
Swiss Alps where saffron had been cultivated since the Middle Ages.

And then, I received an email.

Dear Sylvie, wrote Garcia, *I write to you today on behalf of the
Universal Academy of Cassoulet to ask for your assistance.* His tone
was so formal he might as well have written a letter embossed on
parchment paper. *As I believe you know*, he continued, *the Academy*

is expanding its international reach (!) *and is planning to open embassies around the world. At this point in time, there are embassies in Paris, Tokyo, Quebec and London. I write to you today to let you know that we are now ready for New York.*

I was stunned. He just never stopped. Garcia's faith in the power of cassoulet knew no end.

What he was really looking for, I learned the next day when I reached him by phone, was a chef and a restaurant in New York that would offer 'real' cassoulet (meaning vetted by the Academy) on its menu so that the American public could (finally, he said) learn about the dish and experience the best of the best.

Who was he kidding? Would anybody care? But his enthusiasm and passion were hard to resist, so I called around to chefs and even the French Tourism Office. A week later, I landed in the office of what was then 'Sud de France', a sort of Tourism Board dedicated to the promotion of the southwest of France.

'An embassy for cassoulet in New York? *J'adore!*' exclaimed Marianne Fabre-Lanvin, the director.

By the time we met, I was convinced that the right chef for this tricky task was Philippe Bertineau. Through my work as a food and travel writer I knew many French chefs and restaurateurs, and my native French language allowed for easy communication. A wiry, passionate soul, Bertineau helmed Benoit, the US replica of a Parisian bistro owned by Alain Ducasse, the chef/entrepreneur who, conveniently, also hailed from the southwest of France. I hoped Bertineau would get along with Garcia. Born on a farm in Brittany, he grew up with the solid values and work ethic of the farmland, and I felt they spoke the same language. Both had apprenticed under despots and both believed there were no shortcuts, either in life or in béarnaise.

Over the next few months, the project came to life. Garcia went to Montpellier to meet with the head of Sud de France and came back with two more impressive deals. The Academy would participate in an event in London and would also be part of the upcoming Fête de la Gastronomie in Paris that September.

'We're going to make cassoulet for one hundred and twenty people on top of the Eiffel Tower!' said Garcia, chuckling. And they did!

Bertineau and the Academy corresponded by email, exchanging recipes and mission statements, arguing about the validity of a terroir over another, a cru over another.

One message from the Deputy Secretary read: 'Our rallying cry in Occitan, *aco v'aïmi*, praises our passion for the cassoulet and means "this one I love". We pronounce it *aco baïmi*. Let's make sure to carve out time to rehearse it when we are in New York.'

And so, it happened, that one chilly winter day, twenty members of the Academy landed at JFK.

The local press in Carcassonne covered this unprecedented event with fanfare.

'A 20-person delegation from the Universal Academy of Cassoulet took off this morning bound for New York City to inaugurate the new embassy. Ingredients and *cassoles* were shipped earlier', wrote *L'Indépendant*.

'A memorable evening where the most influential chefs in New York helped induct the chef Philippe Bertineau into the Universal Academy of Cassoulet, an event heralded by the entire American press corps', said *Sud de France Blog*.

'Philippe Bertineau is about to join the select club of French chefs whose mission it is to herald the local specialties of our blessed land', wrote *Le Moci*.

'The defenders of cassoulet storm the Big Apple', heralded *French Morning*.

Due to meet the group at five pm one blustery February afternoon, I showed up early. We hadn't seen each other in about two years, but all Garcia muttered when he saw me was, 'Been waiting, let's go.'

But this time, he was on my turf and I smiled, came close, and kissed him on both cheeks, still amazed he had made the trip. While we walked down Fifth Avenue, I pointed to the various buildings, playing guide until I saw that he was absolutely uninterested. He was tense, and throughout the few days he spent in New York, he only smiled when he was in the restaurant kitchen. That was the only environment where he felt at ease and in control. That was his domain.

Standing at the door in his sparkly whites, Bertineau welcomed him with open arms as if he had been waiting for this moment his entire life, and they embraced. They spent hours prepping, dicing, and hovering over the stock. I watched and listened. Little by little, the members of the group trickled in. One had brought carefully sealed sausages in his suitcase, another had stuffed pig skin in his bag, someone else had smuggled fresh thyme.

On the day of the event, both chefs seemed quite nervous. In the kitchen, no one spoke as bubbly *cassoles* awaited the final heatstroke. French officials, chefs, journalists, and guests arrived as members of the Academy, in red robes and matching berets, assembled in the private salons.

The President of the Academy opened the ceremony, thanked the politicians and proceeded to welcome Bertineau into the Academy. Then, Garcia spoke about the mission of the organization and bestowed the small *cassole* hanging on a ribbon to the chef, who accepted, beaming. A chamber ensemble sounded the trumpets and everyone joined in to sing the hymn to cassoulet. Bubbly wine appeared and soon we were all seated, eagerly awaiting the star of the show.

I pinched myself. Here I was, in Manhattan, as the procession arrived at the door of the dining room. Flashes went off and everyone stood. There were as many *cassoles* as tables and soon we all dug in. Everyone oohed and aahed. The cassoulet was very good but for me there was no new epiphany. My own experience was indelibly linked to the French terroir.

The next day as we said goodbye one more time, Garcia finally embraced me.

'Where should we go next?' he whispered.

26

South of France, July 2011

'ARE WE THERE YET?' MOANED SEVEN-YEAR-OLD TOMMY, only a few minutes after we began the drive from Geneva, bound for a slow journey along France's ancient, mythical *Route des Vacances*, the Nationale 7.

Life had not really allowed me to mourn my father. The night after he died, the only thing I was able to do was wobble towards the kitchen and bake a thin-crust apple tart, his favorite dessert.

Years later, staring at an old photograph of him gripping the wheel of his beloved 1969 Citroën DS with worn-out Hermès gloves, I saw myself at age nine in the back seat, squeezed between my sisters and surrounded by leather suitcases, fishing nets, and beach toys. We were driving the long stretch between Geneva and the sunny Riviera, on our way to la Garoupe on the Cap d'Antibes.

It could have been a quick trip, I reminisced. Most of the

gleaming highway from Paris to Marseille was already built, but even though it boasted the sexy title of *Autoroute du Soleil* (Highway of the Sun), Pâ wouldn't have it. Unlike a boat race, this was about the journey, not the finish line. We would meander on the slow road, the Nationale 7 (also known as N7), with fellow seasonal nomads, along fields of sunflowers and rows of plane trees, shielding us from the pointed sun.

The concept of paid vacations for the working population emerged in France after 1936, when the Front Populaire, a leftist coalition, ruled the country. The concept of *Les Grandes Vacances* became a pillar of French society. During the summer weeks, millions descended on the South, drawn by the soothing song of cicadas swinging in the balmy nights, lavender clouds, and rosemary-infused legs of lamb.

Every French road deemed 'Nationale' takes its source on the steps of Notre Dame Cathedral in Paris, and the N7, built on an ancient Roman Viae, ends in Menton at the Italian border. Over the years, the road became a symbol of sunny libertine freedom but also delicious halts, as restaurants, bakeries, and gourmet shops sprang up along the two-lane silver ribbon.

In the summer of 2011, I piled up my own family in a rented car and set to retrace my steps for a food and travel story. Would we have fun? I wondered. Would we gain ten pounds each? Could I create for my children lifelong memories that matched mine? Would the trip confirm that my passion for France, food, and discovery stemmed from these summer road trips? Would I catch glimpses of the father I so missed? I resolved to try.

In my youth, our itinerary was always the same, but in 2011 I decided to sketch my own *route gourmande* and taste the regional specialties along the way. Our first stop was Pâtisserie Labully in Saint Genix, about an hour from Geneva.

Many legends surround the birth of the gâteau Labully, a shapely brioche studded with pralines and sculpted, as rumor has it, to suggest the breast of Saint Agathe. A bit heady from the aroma of orange blossom water, I watched Zoe tear chunks of the sweet bread tinted with crimson tongues of sugar, and suck on them.

Back in the car, giddy on sweets and nostalgia, I unfolded the Michelin map like a tablecloth on my lap. We would join the N7 in Lyon, my grandmother Madeleine's hometown, the self-proclaimed world capital of gastronomy.

'Three rivers flow through Lyon,' my father used to say, rehashing an old adage, 'Le Rhône, la Saône and le Beaujolais!'

We arrived in time for lunch and headed to Brasserie Georges, an old-time family favorite art-deco eatery which boasts *Bonne Bière et Bonne Chère depuis 1836* (good food and good beer since 1836) on the stucco walls. I had read that Jules Verne, Edith Piaf, and even Ernest Hemingway had dined there but, seated amongst the bustling crowd, my adventurous Zoe was unimpressed. She ordered steak tartare and stared, with eyes as large as the plate, while the dynamic old-school waitress, clad in a formal white apron over a black dress, launched an acrobatic juggle of capers, onions, pickles, and raw egg, blending them so fast that no 'but I don't like …' could even be formulated before a red orb landed in front of the child, who dove in fork first and uttered what would become the refrain of our journey: 'hmmmm'. There was no cassoulet on the menu – we were miles away from Carcassonne after all – but I ordered a Lyon delicacy, a fatty *saucisson pistaché*, and sighed as a nutty layer of pleasure coated my tongue with what felt like the languorous taste of France.

'Stop!' I yelled, on our way to Vienne the next day, as I glimpsed the first red-and-white Nationale 7 cement road marker. Michael, thinking we'd hit something, screeched the car to a halt. I got out and ran back towards the marker. I hadn't seen one of those in more than thirty years.

Under what looked like a weathered headstone slept my childhood and my story, and, yes, somehow, my father too. By the time I pulled myself away, my tears had soaked the old stone. It was time, though; Fernand Point was waiting.

I'd first heard about Chef Fernand Point, who died in 1955, from my maternal grandparents: his laugh, his bonhomie as large as his waist, the champagne magnums he polished off throughout the day, the *pâté en croûte*. During my interview with Paul Bocuse, the chef had reminisced about his mentor and what it had meant to work as an apprentice in the kitchen that, in 1933, would be the first to be awarded three Michelin stars. When we parked next to La Pyramide, the Roman monument for which the restaurant was named, my heart was pounding. After passing to Fernand Point's wife, and then later to his daughter, the restaurant had been sold and reopened under a new chef.

But that meal taught me a different lesson, proving how futile it was to attempt to recreate what is gone. Even though the food was pleasant, I couldn't find anything in the new chef's world of flavors that spoke of Point to me. I was searching for the past, but Point and his era were gone for good.

The next morning, as we drove along the steep banks of the Rhône, trimmed with sun-thirsty vineyards, an intense tawny aroma suddenly invaded the car. No serious chocoholic (or parent) can drive through Tain-l'Hermitage – site of some of the worst traffic jams I remembered – without a stop at the Valrhona shop, next to the original chocolate factory. It took Zoe and Tommy almost an hour to taste, hesitate, negotiate, and finally choose which bonbons, bars, and truffles we would pick.

Later on, I recognized my truck stop of choice: La Mule, with its familiar red and blue sign of 'Les Routiers', the national association of truck drivers, created in 1934. We stood at the entrance for a while, waiting for a table.

'How long has there been a restaurant here?' I asked a flushed waitress.

'No clue,' she yelled over the happy buzz. 'Since 1900 maybe?'

I took it all in: the regional accents, the rosy, creased faces, the rotund paunches bumping against rustic wooden tables, the humongous bottles of red and rosé that appeared as soon as we sat down, and the all-you-can-eat hors d'oeuvres buffet holding shredded carrots, beef muzzle salad, canned sardines, and a rainbow of pâtés. Here was the simple, joyous France I wanted to baste in, full of geniality and appetite.

We passed the celebrated chef Anne-Sophie Pic's three-star temple, set literally on the Nationale 7, in the exact spot where her grandfather André relocated his inn in 1936. As soon as I spotted a road sign for Montélimar, my tongue automatically reverted to wiggling through my back teeth in an attempt to scrape off any fleck of nougat stuck there. As a kid, even a simple refueling stop in the area meant we would stock up on the honeyed, nutty paste.

The next day, it was a challenge to get the kids up and ready early to watch the launch of an antique car rally in nearby Piolenc, the self-anointed capital of garlic. Thankfully our host, fourth-generation vintner Jean-Pierre Serguier, who runs the Chateau Simian vineyard, had prepared the kind of breakfast that smoothed over any grumpy kid: *pains au chocolat*, dry *saucisson* and fresh grape juice, the color of clear dawn.

'Finally, a wine I like,' exclaimed Tommy, convinced he'd discovered rosé. Rather than stay in Avignon, we dodged the crowds and crossed the wide Rhône towards rocky, medieval Villeneuve-lès-Avignon. In a fragrant, ancient garden stood Le Prieuré, one of my parents' favorite haunts, where that night at the table, a beaming Zoe was called *mademoiselle* for the first time.

The following day, only a mile away at the Guinguette du Vieux Moulin, an open-air eatery on the banks of the river, I felt we had landed in Renoir's *Luncheon of the Boating Party*, minus the straw hats.

Everywhere along the road, the past sizzled just under the surface: 'In 1968,' said owner Jean-André Charial, 'my grandfather advertised a free tank of gas to entice travelers off the Nationale 7 to our hotel, L'Oustau de Baumanière.' We admired the soaring, lacy rocks, the crumbling citadel of Les Baux, and enjoyed Charial's excellent cuisine infused by herbs from the garden. Another day and, just as it was years ago, I was the first to glimpse the Mediterranean. '*La mer!*' I exclaimed, scaring the whole gang. We drove through the rusty Esterel range and finally arrived at the Cap d'Antibes. The pull was too strong to resist. I abandoned ship, leaving my husband to check in and, alone with my memories, ran the few steps down to the sea, struggling to breathe normally. Was the familiar, tannic eucalyptus scent choking me? It was the end of the day, and at the cafes that ringed the beach, waiters dragged on their cigarettes as they piled up the black-and-white woven bistro chairs.

Then I saw the monumental gate and, beyond, the vacations of my childhood. Towards the sea, the rocky cape enclosed the grounds, stretching towards the horizon. An incongruous cement path now ran alongside the new high wall, but the magical garden refused to be contained. Cypresses rose above, solid and thick as plumes; giant bougainvillea spilled as if bowing to me. Further, where the white waves wavered, towering umbrella pines sketched their inky silhouette on a paling sky.

Behind that wall? My tricycle on the gravel taking me through rows of sunny mimosas; my grandmother sitting under the ancestral wisteria; chalky steps leading to the sea; peach juice dripping from my chin onto the craggy white rocks. Would the stains still show?

The next day, we headed to Menton and its famous lemon groves – the end of the route. We drove through Nice and above Eze, with perhaps the most stunning coastal views anywhere in the world. Lining the Nationale 7, palm trees had replaced the *platanes* of the north. On the other side of the now-useless customs barrack, Italy beckoned.

'Where now?' asked Tommy.

'Home,' I answered, hoping he wouldn't ask where that was. He didn't, and we turned around.

27

New York, December 2011

THERE WAS NO USE IN TRYING TO MAKE CASSOULET AT home in New York anymore. I understood that beyond the battle between partridge and duck, beans and haricots verts, the elusive taste of 'home' couldn't be replicated away from its original terroir.

Later that year, Daniel Boulud hired me to work on a massive cookbook. This book, his own anthology of French cuisine, would keep me busy for two years. As the main writer, I spent hours traipsing after and shadowing him in the kitchen, in the dining room and around his many restaurants. At home, I attempted to replicate many of the recipes we were developing. I cooked sea bass and carrot essence, veal rack and even a chocolate bomb. I was fascinated by the populous choreography of his restaurant kitchens, some almost as large as a New York block – worlds away from Domaine Balthazar and its windows framed by climbing roses, with Garcia at the stove and Guy everywhere else.

The cookbook came out in September 2013 and became a calling card of sorts. I hadn't been in touch with anyone in Carcassonne, but I often thought about the family and sent a holiday card. I didn't hear back, and another year went by.

By 2014, my marriage showed so many cracks that, similar to an antique Chinese teapot, it finally broke into myriad pieces. One sad July afternoon, I moved out of our family home, and after fifteen years found myself living on my own. The children were spending every other week with me, and in those early times, I cooked constantly – my way of coping, and loving.

That fall, I was researching the city of Toulouse and its new chefs when someone mentioned that Guy Garcia was working independently. I made a few calls, afraid to call Eric directly. What had happened?

'You haven't heard?' asked a member of the Academy. 'He and Guy had a terrible fight one evening and Guy left the next morning before dawn with his wife and the kids. The restaurant is for sale.'

I was stunned. How could that be? That family seemed so much tighter than my family of origin, certainly tighter than the family I had tried and failed to build. Laurence said that cassoulet kept them together. Who had broken the crust? I was devastated, but didn't dare call the chef. Their fracture wasn't mine.

Then I heard that Philippe Bertineau, chef of the New York Embassy, had left Benoit and started cooking at an American eatery. I felt as if the winds of change were blowing away my carefully constructed world.

It seemed as good a time as any to get a DNA testing. That way, I thought, I would finally know where my Sephardic ancestry came from. But when the results came back, they were implacable.

I was 99.8 percent Ashkenazi, meaning from Eastern Europe. The Mediterranean had been a dream. The concept of home was more elusive than ever.

A few months later, I accepted a Friday night dinner invitation to the home of friends who were practicing Orthodox Jews. After Ruth lit the Shabbat candles and her husband blessed the wine and the golden challah, they proceeded to serve us from a large pot on the stove. To my surprise, heaps of beans, simmered onions and chunks of fragrant veal shank landed on my plate. The aroma was familiar, a sort of grassy, earthy scent that gave me goosebumps.

'What?' asked Ruth, seeing my face. 'You don't like cholent?'

Oh, but I did. I loved it. On my tongue, I tasted something akin to cassoulet.

That very night, I dug into my food encyclopedia and read that cholent or tcholent, the Eastern European Shabbat stew, was perhaps the most emblematic dish of the Ashkenazi Jewish repertoire. In her iconic cookbook, *The Book of Jewish Food*, Claudia Roden relates that in the shtetl of yesteryear, the stew was often started twenty-four hours before the day of rest and sealed with a flour and water dough before the women brought the pot to the baker's oven where it simmered all night. There would be a warm dish, but no need to cook on the Shabbat. That was awfully similar to the stories Garcia had told. A different day of rest, different meats, different people but the same concept, the same search for comfort.

Roden described the historical emotional significance of cholent, its aroma permeating the houses of the shtetl. The name cholent, she explained, probably came from the ancient French words *chault*, meaning hot, and *lent*, meaning slow. Cholent, I read in her book, as well as in the writings of food historian Gil Marks, was most probably the precursor of cassoulet. Even the author

Joan Nathan writes in her wonderful *King Solomon's Table* that the overnight Sabbath stew is 'suspiciously similar to cassoulet'.

๛

Looking back to my quest, I saw clearly that cassoulet was the clue, but it was never the revelation. Led by my love for Garcia and his family, I uncovered a world of traditions and flavors that fascinated me. But I now understood that their world wasn't mine. Because I was in the South of France and because I was convinced that part of my heritage was Sephardic and Mediterranean, I had linked the taste of 'home' to my surroundings. What I failed to understand was that the dish itself was a remnant of my Eastern European tradition. The odd feeling of home nestled in that first bite of cassoulet was in fact the taste memory of my ancestors. The identity I was searching for, the certainty of who I was, had no connection with geography or passports.

My home is neither in New York nor in Carcassonne or Geneva. Home is who I am, not where I am. My home, I discovered, is my Judaism, with its history, traditions and, yes, its cuisine. Over the next few years, I would find my true inner home and the man who held its key. My Judaism would lead me home. In truth, there is no physical home. Only people linked together by history and culture. And hunger.

Recipes

Please note that the recipes in this book were only cooked in conventional ovens. The general rule tells us that if using a fan-forced or convection oven to reduce the temperature by 20°C (70°F).

This book uses 15 ml (½ fl oz) tablespoons. Cooks using 20 ml (¾ fl oz) tablespoons should be mindful of slightly reducing the amount with their tablespoon measurements. Metric cup measurements are used, i.e., 250 ml (8½ fl oz) for 1 cup. In the US a cup is 237 ml (8 fl oz), so American cooks should be generous with their cup measurements; in the UK, a cup is 284 ml (9½ fl oz), so British cooks should be scant.

Cassoulet adapted from Eric Garcia's

❦ *YIELD: Serves 8* ❦
TIME: 7¹/₂ hours over 3 days

This recipe is made over three days. On the first day you prepare the stock and soak the beans; on the second day you cook the meats and assemble the cassoulet. The last day, the day of eating, you cook the cassoulet one last time.

1 kg (2 lb 3 oz) dried lingot or other large white beans

1 pig trotter

300 g (11 oz/1 ¼ cups) fresh pork rind, cut into strips

1 ham bone

1 fresh ham hock

1 bouquet garni (tie together 1 celery stalk, 4 thyme sprigs, 4 parsley sprigs, 3 bay leaves)

10 cloves

1 tablespoon coarse salt

1 tablespoon duck fat

250 g (9 oz/1 cup) fresh pork belly, cut into cubes

1 medium onion, chopped

2 garlic bulbs (about 100 g/3 ½ oz), cloves peeled and crushed

450 g (1 lb) fresh garlic pork sausage, cut into 7 cm (3 in) long pieces

4 legs duck confit

Day I

1. Sort through the beans to remove any broken ones.

2. Rinse the beans thoroughly and soak overnight in cold water.

3. In a large stock pot, combine the pig trotter, pork rind, ham bone and hock, bouquet garni, cloves, and salt. Cover with water (about 3 liters/101 fl oz/12 cups). Bring to a boil and simmer, covered, for 2 hours.

4. Let the stock cool, then remove the meats and discard the ham bone. Remove the bouquet garni and wring it out into the stock pot. Pour the stock through a sieve into a storage container. Refrigerate stock and meats separately overnight.

Day 2

5. Drain the beans and rinse under cold water. Bring a large pot of water to a boil. Blanch the beans in boiling water for 7 minutes, then drain.

6. Debone the trotter and ham hock. Cut the meat into chunks.

7. In a large pot, bring the stock and the beans to a boil, then simmer for about 30 minutes over a low heat. Drain the beans, reserving the stock and place the beans in a bowl.

8. Meanwhile, melt the duck fat in a large pan. Add the pork belly cubes and brown on all sides. Remove from the pan with a slotted spoon and set aside. In the same pan, sauté the onion and garlic over a medium–low heat until translucent. Stir constantly to avoid burning. Remove from the pan with a slotted spoon, add to the beans and stir until well coated.

9. In the same pan, brown the sausage pieces, then remove and set aside. Sear the duck confit to melt its fat. Debone the duck legs when cool enough to handle.

10. Preheat the oven to 160°C (320°F).

11. To assemble the cassoulet, spread half the beans at the bottom of a *cassole* or large Dutch oven. Then layer the sausage pieces, the duck confit and the pork meats, and cover with the rest of the beans and then with the stock. Bake uncovered for about 2 hours. Check regularly to break the crust, making sure it doesn't look dry; add stock or water as necessary. Bubbles should appear around the edges. Remove from the oven and let the *cassole* rest until cool, then refrigerate overnight, keeping remaining stock if any.

Day 3

12. About 3 hours before serving, take the *cassole* out of the refrigerator and bring to room temperature (this will take about 45 minutes).

13. Preheat the oven to 160°C (320°F).

14. Add about 250 ml (9 oz/1 cup) stock or water to the *cassole* and bake for 2 hours, breaking the crust regularly. Make sure the stew remains moist by adding stock or water as needed.

15. Remove from the oven and serve family style.

Le Cassoulet de Castelnaudary

You can prepare the stock on day one and reserve in the fridge until ready
to cook the beans on day two.

1 kg (2 lb 5 oz) dried Tarbais
  beans or other large white beans
8 garlic cloves, peeled (5 crushed
  and 3 left whole)
100 g (¼ lb) pancetta, diced
250 g (½ lb) fresh pork rind,
  cut into large strips
1 pork trotter
1 fresh ham hock
1 carrot, peeled
1 large onion, peeled and pinned
  with 1 clove
1 leek
1 celery stalk
3 or 4 thyme sprigs and 3 bay
  leaves tied together
1½ tablespoons coarse sea salt
freshly ground black pepper

1½ tablespoons tomato paste
5 legs duck confit
400 g (1 lb) pork spare ribs
  (about 8 separated ribs)
450 g (1 lb) fresh garlic pork
  sausage, cut into 7 cm (3 in)
  long pieces

Day 1

1. Rinse the beans thoroughly and soak overnight in cold water.

Day 2

2. Drain the beans, place in a pot and cover with cold water. Bring to a boil and blanch for 5 minutes. Drain.

3. Combine the five crushed garlic cloves with the diced pancetta. Set aside.

4. In a large stock pot, place the pork rind strips, trotter, ham hock, carrot, onion with clove, leek, celery, tied thyme and bay leaves, two garlic cloves, and the garlic pancetta mixture. Cover with water (about 4 liters/4.5 quarts) and add the salt and pepper. Bring to a boil and simmer for 2 hours.

5. Once cool enough to handle, strain the stock into another large stock pot. Reserve the pork rind strips and trotter; discard the rest. There should be about 3.5 liters (118 fl oz/14 cups) of stock.

6. Add the beans to the stock. The beans should be covered by the stock; if not, add more water. Mix in the tomato paste, bring to a boil and simmer partially covered for 1½ – 2 hours. The beans should be tender but not mushy. Drain the beans and reserve the stock.

7. While the beans are cooking, melt the fat of the duck confit legs and brown in a large skillet, then set aside. In the same skillet, brown the pork ribs, then remove and repeat with the sausage. Add duck fat as needed to prevent burning. When the duck legs are cool enough to handle, pull the meat away from the bones in large chunks and discard the bones. Reserve remaining duck fat.

8. Preheat oven to 160°C (320°F).

9. Cut the last garlic clove in half and rub the inside of the *cassole* with it (a heavy, wide-mouthed 4–5 liter (135–169 fl oz/16–21 cups) Dutch oven or clay pot about 10 cm (4 in) high will do).

10. On the bottom of the *cassole*, lay the pork rind strips flat, then add the trotter meat and half the beans. Add the duck meat and top with the remainder of the beans. Push the sausage pieces and the ribs into the beans. Add the reserved fat from the skillet and half the reserved stock. Add freshly ground pepper generously all over the top.

11. Cook for about 3 hours. Bubbles should appear around the edges; if not, add stock as needed. Break the crust regularly with a spoon and let it form again.

12. Remove from the oven and cool before refrigerating overnight.

Day 3

13. About 3 hours before serving, take the *cassole* out of the refrigerator and bring to room temperature (this will take about 45 minutes).

14. Preheat the oven to 160°C (320°F) and bake the cassoulet for 2 hours. Make sure the beans don't dry out and add water as needed. Break the crust again two or three times without crushing the beans.

15. Remove from the oven. Allow the cassoulet to rest for 10 minutes, then serve family style, directly from the *cassole* in the center of the table.

Le Cassoulet de Toulouse

⚚ *YIELD: Serves 8* ⚚
TIME: 9¹/₂ hours over 2 days

While this recipe can be prepared and served within one day, it is best to cook on day one, refrigerate overnight, then bake for an additional 2 hours prior to serving.

900 g (2 lb) dried Tarbais beans
   or other large white beans
6 garlic cloves (3 whole and
   3 crushed)
20 rainbow peppercorns
10 cloves
1 large piece (about 250 g/9 oz)
   fresh pork rind, rinsed
1 bouquet garni (tie together
   1 thyme sprig, 1 bay leaf,
   5 curly parsley sprigs,
   1 celery stalk, 1 leek)
1 carrot, chopped
3 onions, peeled (1 left whole
   and 2 finely chopped)
200 g (7 oz) tomato puree
1 tablespoon tomato paste
1½ tablespoons coarse sea salt
freshly ground black pepper

450 g (1 lb) fresh garlic pork
   sausage, cut into 7 cm (3 in)
   long pieces
250 g (½ lb) fresh pork belly,
   cubed
4 legs duck confit
1.2 kg (2 lb 10 oz) boneless lamb
   shoulder, cubed
1 tablespoon duck fat
200 g (7 oz) breadcrumbs
   (half if you only bake the
   cassoulet once)

Day 1

1. Rinse the beans thoroughly, then soak for at least 4 hours and no longer than 12 hours.

2. Drain the beans under cold water, then blanch in a large pot of boiling water for 5 minutes. Drain, then rinse under cold water again.

3. Using a piece of cheesecloth, make a bundle with the whole garlic cloves, the peppercorns and the cloves.

4. Place the pork rind at the bottom of a large stock pot. Add the beans, the bouquet garni, the tied cheesecloth, the carrot and the whole onion. Cover with water (about 2 liters/68 fl oz/8 cups). Mix in the tomato puree and tomato paste, and add the salt and pepper. Bring to a boil and simmer for 1 hour. Skim the surface when necessary.

5. Add the sausage and continue to cook for another 30 minutes, then remove the sausage and set aside. Drain the beans over a large bowl, reserving the cooking liquid. Discard the pork rind, bouquet garni and cheesecloth. Add salt to taste if necessary.

6. In the meantime, blanch the pieces of pork belly in salted boiling water for 10 minutes. Drain and set aside.

7. Brown the duck legs in a frying pan, skin side first over a medium heat for about 7 minutes then set aside. In the same pan, brown the lamb pieces on all sides, then set aside. Still using the same pan and fat (if necessary, add 1 teaspoon of the duck fat) lower the heat to medium–low and cook the chopped onions and the garlic until translucent – about 8 minutes.

8. Add the onions and the garlic to the beans and mix well.

9. When cool enough to handle, take the meat off the duck legs and leave in chunks.

Assemble the cassoulet

10. Preheat oven to 120°C (250°F).

11. Spread the duck fat on the interior of a *cassole* or large Dutch oven.

12. Layer one-third of the beans at the bottom with half of the meats (lamb, pork belly, sausage and duck). Repeat, then top with the last third of the beans. Add four ladles of the cooking liquid, then sprinkle half of the breadcrumbs over the top.

13. Bake for 4 hours. The cassoulet should be bubbling around the top. Regularly break the crust with a spoon, making sure the cassoulet stays moist. Add more cooking liquid if necessary.

14. At this point, you can either serve the cassoulet or refrigerate it overnight for a second bake (recommended).

Day 2

15. About 3 hours before serving, take the *cassole* out of the refrigerator and bring to room temperature (this will take about 45 minutes).

16. Preheat the oven to 160°C (320°F) and cook the cassoulet for another 2 hours. Once the sides bubble, start breaking the crust. Add water as necessary. Halfway through, top with the remaining breadcrumbs.

17. Let it cool for 10 minutes and serve family style directly from the *cassole*.

Sylvie's Cassoulet

YIELD: Serves 8

TIME: 11 hours over 2 days

Don't be intimidated by the number of hours required to cook a cassoulet. This is not a complicated recipe to follow, and there is only about an hour of prep time. This stew, adapted from Etienne Rousselot's, is all about slow cooking and, because every stew tastes better the day after it has been made, chefs and cooks recommend making it over two days. In this recipe the beans are neither pre-cooked nor soaked in advance.

1 kg (2 lb 3 oz) dried Tarbais or
   other large white beans

4 fresh ham hocks

3 large onions, peeled and
   quartered

5 thyme sprigs

1 ½ tablespoons coarse sea salt

freshly ground black pepper

150 g (5 oz) fresh pork rind,
   cut into 5 cm (2 in) cubes

1 ham bone

1 large garlic bulb, cloves peeled

1 tablespoon duck fat

450 g (1 lb) fresh garlic pork
   sausage, cut into 7 cm (3 in)
   long pieces

4 legs duck confit

¼ teaspoon freshly grated
   nutmeg

Day I

1. Rinse the beans thoroughly, discard little stones if any, then set aside.

2. In a large stock pot, place the ham hocks with one onion, the thyme sprigs, 1 tablespoon salt and a good grind of pepper. Cover with water and bring to a boil over a high heat. Reduce heat to medium–low and simmer, partially covered, for 2 hours. (While cooking you may start on step 3.) Remove from heat and allow to cool for about 15 minutes. Remove the ham hocks from the stock, tear off the meat and set aside. Discard the onion, thyme, skin, fat and bones. Reserve stock.

3. While the ham hocks are cooking, place the pork rind, the ham bone and one onion in a large, heavy-based pot. Cook over medium heat, stirring frequently, for about 20 minutes, or until the pork rinds become translucent.

4. Add the beans to the pork rind mixture, and enough water to cover (about 2 liters/68 fl oz/8 cups). Bring to a simmer and reduce heat to low until the beans are tender (about 1 hour and 15 minutes). Ensure the beans remain submerged; add water as needed.

5. Set aside to cool. You should have at least 4 cups of the bean cooking liquid. Combine with leftover reserved stock.

6. In a blender, add the last onion, the whole garlic cloves and ½ cup of water. Puree until smooth. Set aside.

7. Melt the duck fat in a large skillet over medium–high heat. Cook the sausages, stirring frequently until brown, about 10 minutes. Add the garlic/onion puree and reduce heat to medium–low. Sauté, turning the sausages occasionally, for another 10 minutes.

8. Preheat oven to 175°C (350°F).

9. With a slotted spoon, remove and discard the ham bone and the onion from the beans. Then transfer half the beans with the pork

rind to a *cassole* (a heavy 5–6 liter (169–202 fl oz/21–23 cups) Dutch oven will work as well).

10. Layer the ham meat over the beans, then the sausages and garlic puree and spread evenly. Arrange the duck legs on top.

11. Add the remaining beans. Season with the nutmeg and add just enough stock to cover the beans (about 750 ml/25 fl oz/3 cups). Reserve remaining stock for later use.

12. Bake uncovered for about 1 hour, until the cassoulet comes to a simmer and a crust begins to form.

13. Reduce heat to 120°C (250°F) and cook for 3 more hours. Regularly check and press down the top with the back of a spoon to break the crust and bring fresh beans to the surface. Add stock to keep cassoulet bubbling around the edges.

14. Remove the cassoulet from the oven and allow to cool before refrigerating overnight, covered. Refrigerate any remaining stock.

Day 2

15. Remove cassoulet from the refrigerator and allow to come to room temperature (about 45 minutes). Warm up the stock. Preheat the oven to 175°C (350°F).

16. Bake for about 1 hour, until cassoulet comes to a simmer and crust begins to form again. Add stock as needed. Cassoulet should be bubbling along the edges and feel moist with a crust on top.

17. Reduce heat to 120°C (250°F) and bake for another 3 hours, breaking the crust regularly with the back of a spoon and adding liquid as necessary (if no stock remains, add water).

18. Remove the cassoulet from the oven and let it rest for 15 minutes before serving. Place the *cassole* at the center of the table and serve family style.

Sylvie's Cholent

YIELD: Serves 8

TIME: prep 30 mins, cooking time 10 hours

500 g (1 lb 2 oz) dried Tarbais beans or other large white beans

2 kg (4 lb) first-cut beef brisket, trimmed and cut in 5 cm (2 in) cubes

4 chicken legs, thighs and drumsticks separated

3 tablespoons coarse sea salt

freshly ground black pepper

2 tablespoons chicken or duck fat

2 large onions, peeled and chopped

3 garlic cloves, peeled and crushed

60 g (2 oz/¼ cup) curly parsley, finely chopped

60 g (2 oz/¼ cup) fresh thyme leaves

2 tablespoons sweet Hungarian paprika

¼ teaspoon allspice

2 tablespoons honey

185 g (6 lb ½ oz/¾ cup) pearl barley

2 marrow bones (about 5 cm/ 2 in thick)

6 medium potatoes, peeled and quartered

4 carrots, peeled and diced

1 small butternut squash, peeled and diced

optional (if in season): chestnuts, cooked and peeled

8 large eggs

1. Rinse the beans thoroughly and soak for at least 2 hours in cold water, then drain.

2. Bring a large pot of water to a boil. Blanch the beans in boiling water for 15 minutes, then drain and set aside.

3. Preheat oven to 90°C (200°F).

4. Season both meats with 1 tablespoon of salt and a good grind of pepper.

5. In a large ovenproof pot with a tight lid, melt the chicken or duck fat. Sear the brisket cubes on all sides, then remove and reserve. Sear the chicken on all sides. Remove and reserve.

6. Using the same pot, sauté the onions and the garlic over a low heat.

7. Stir in the parsley, thyme, paprika, 1½ tablespoons salt, allspice and honey. Stir for 1–2 minutes.

8. Add the beans and the pearl barley. Stir until well coated.

9. Add the meats and the marrow bones on top.

10. Add the potatoes, carrots and squash, and chestnuts if using, as a layer over the meats and marrow bones.

11. Wedge the eggs in their shells between the potatoes and squash.

12. Add enough water to cover. Add ½ tablespoon of coarse sea salt, then bring to a boil.

13. Cover and bake in the oven for 10 hours.

14. Remove and serve from the pot.

Gateway Cassoulet

TIME: prep 40 mins, cooking time 2^{1}/2 hours

I will probably get a lot of flak for this recipe. 'What?! You've taken us through this entire exercise and now you're giving us a recipe that is not authentic?' I know, I know, but I call it Gateway for a reason. As a nice entry-level weekday cassoulet, this is not bad. Try it, tweak it, double it for your friends, and then, when you are ready, go tackle the real thing!

500 g (1 lb 2 oz) dried cannellini
   beans or other large white beans

1 large onion, peeled and quartered

8 garlic cloves, peeled

1 parsley sprig (leaves only)

3 thyme sprigs (leaves only)

½ tablespoon salt

350 g (12 oz) fresh pork belly with
   skin, cut into 3 cm (1 in) cubes

1 tablespoon duck fat

200 g (½ lb) fresh pork sausage,
   cut into 5 cm (2 in) long pieces

2 legs duck confit

1 carrot, peeled and chopped

¼ teaspoon freshly grated nutmeg

freshly ground black pepper

1 liter (34 fl oz/4 cups)
   store-bought chicken stock

1. Rinse the beans thoroughly, then soak for at least 2 hours but no longer than 12 hours.
2. Preheat oven to 175°C (350°F).
3. Drain the beans and rinse under cold water. Fill a 4 liter (135 fl oz/ 16 cups) Dutch oven with water and bring to a boil. Blanch the beans in the boiling water for 7 minutes, then drain and run under cold water again. Set aside in a bowl.

4. In a blender, combine the onion, garlic, parsley, thyme, salt and 60 ml (2 fl oz/¼ cup) of water. Puree until smooth.

5. In the Dutch oven, sear the pork belly cubes over medium heat until browned on all sides – about 5 minutes. Stir often to prevent burning. Remove and set aside.

6. Melt the duck fat in the Dutch oven over medium heat, then cook the sausage, stirring frequently until brown – about 5 minutes. Remove the sausage and set aside, then add the duck legs and sear for about 1 minute per side. Remove and set aside. Add the garlic/onion puree and reduce heat to low. Cook for 10 minutes, stirring regularly and scraping any pieces of meat stuck to the bottom.

7. Add the puree to the beans, along with the carrot, and mix until well coated.

8. Transfer about one-third of the bean mix to the Dutch oven, enough to cover the bottom.

9. Layer the pork belly over the beans, then the sausages. Finally, place the duck legs on top and cover with the remaining beans. Season with the nutmeg and a good grind of pepper. Add just enough stock to cover the beans. Reserve any remaining stock to add during the cooking process.

10. Bake uncovered until the cassoulet comes to a simmer on the sides and a crust begins to form – about 40 minutes. Reduce heat to 150°C (300°F) and cook for 1 hour 45 minutes, checking regularly to break the crust with the back of a spoon and ensure that the cassoulet remains moist. Add stock or water if necessary.

11. Remove the cassoulet from the oven and let it rest for 15 minutes before serving. Place the Dutch oven at the center of the table and serve family style.

Acknowledgements

This book would not have happened had the late Michael Batterberry, co-founder and editor-in-chief of Food Arts, not commissioned me to write an article about the history of cassoulet and I am very grateful to him.

To my family, and especially my two children, thank you for your patience while I hammered yet another draft of *Cassoulet Confessions* – you both make me so proud.

I am deeply indebted to the founder, chefs, and members of Carcassonne's *Académie Universelle du Cassoulet*, who opened their kitchen, their arms, and their hearts to me.

My dear Valerie Gladstone, gone way too soon, believed in this book before I did. I am so lucky she was my friend.

Editor extraordinaire Sophie Laissue is a gentle, brilliant guide. I am grateful to my friend Carole Bonstein for introducing us and believing this cassoulet obsession could amount to something.

Over the years, family and friends became supportive early readers. Thank you so much for your precious help: Stephanie Abou, Brigitte Bigar, Annie-Claire Blum, Daniel Boulud, Paula de la Cruz, Philicia Endelman, Miguel Esteban, Marianne Fabre-Lanvin, Georgette Farkas, Alexii Friedman, Elizabeth Giret-Bertrand, Marie Hasse, Chris Hunt, Yvette Icher, Marianne Jensen, Libby Johnson, Ann Jungmeyer, Eric Latsky, Lesley Leben, Michelle Palmer-Boulud, Carolyn Perla, Ryan Poynter, Ginger Saariaho, James Sturz, and Kathleen Wallace.

Thank you, Dorothy Kalins and Roger Sherman for your support, advice and friendship.

Thank you, Joan Nathan for welcoming me into your home to discuss the connections between cholent and cassoulet. Thank you to Harvey Weiss, friend, artist and early reader, for your wonderful illustration.

I am lucky to have François Garai's scholar's eye and unwavering support, as well as Gregori Volokhine's friendship and keen literary mind. I am grateful for Stephen Vann's sharp eye and for pushing me to find my voice, hidden under the cassoulet crust.

What a treat it was to work with Marion Sultan as we tested yet one more cassoulet recipe!

At Hardie Grant, thanks to Chef Jenn Louis, I found a wonderful publishing family. Thank you so much Kasi Collins, Jane Grant, Antonietta Melideo, Roxy Ryan, Kristin Thomas, Jane Willson and Joanna Wong.

Thank you Deb Shapiro, Suzanne Williams, and Katherine Stroud for your precious support, Vanessa Lanaway for her brilliant queries and to Emily O'Neill for a cover that encapsulates my story so well.